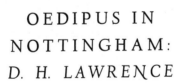

OEDIPUS IN
NOTTINGHAM:
D. H. LAWRENCE

OEDIPUS IN NOTTINGHAM:
D. H. LAWRENCE

By Daniel A. Weiss ✓   ✓   ✓   ✓   ✓

Seattle · 1962
UNIVERSITY OF WASHINGTON PRESS

FOREWORD

WHILE THE MOST articulate criticism of our day has been formalistic, finding literature autonomous and the writing of it an escape from personality, this view has not gone unchallenged. Another has jostled it, unabashedly holding that literature is autobiographical. This second kind is too sophisticated to assume, as it is often accused of doing, that external events in the artist's life have an immediate and simple relation to his books. Instead it enlarges autobiography to include the mind's motivating centers, some of them unconscious. It admits that writers transform their raw material, but asks what impulsions or choices underlie the transformation. It does not deny the formalist argument that writers are affected by literary tradition and by literary forms which they have not invented; it argues, however, that even when traditional forms are used they are not adopted dispassionately but are fitted, by their insistencies or constraints, to the minds that take them up.

While modern writers have inspired both critical camps, most of them have tended, in private at least, to see their art in the second way as the working out of obsessive images. Such a formulation is of course heavily influenced by the age of psychology in which they find themselves. The strong influence of Hartleyan psychology on Romantic poets was mild compared to the influence of Freud and Jung on contemporary writers. Freudian theory, particularly, has come to fill so dominating a place that it has superseded classical mythology as the shared core of knowledge that author and reader expect of each other. Today we hear about the Oedipus complex before we learn about Oedipus. This psychology has affected even those who do not accept it; they feel forced to attack it, to diverge from it, or in other ways to concede that it is a key point of reference even for them.

D. H. Lawrence is an extraordinary example of the writer who searches his own mind and jerrybuilds a psychology which he later defends against Freud and Jung. He was like a patient who reads all the literature on his malady, writes some of it even, and doctors himself. A knowledge of Lawrence's simples can clarify his complicated relation to his own books.

Daniel Weiss approaches Lawrence with two advantages rarely found in company: an expert acquaintance with modern psychology, and a keen sense of those elements in literature, such as style and the sense of external reality, which do not yield much to psychological analysis. He is thoroughly aware of the objections to his method which formalistic critics make, and he takes account of them. This sense of discretion makes his writing more persuasive.

Necessarily he deals at length with Lawrence's Oedipus complex, the most famous such complex in literature since Dostoevski's. But to name these two writers together is to recognize how individual such universal complexes can be. Mr. Weiss succeeds in showing the individuality of Lawrence's wrestlings with his impulses, as the struggle proceeds in novels which Lawrence preferred to call "thought-adventures." He demonstrates, too, that characters in the novels who are assumed to be modeled on actual people, as Gerald Crich in *Women in Love* resembles Middleton Murry, became elements in the fantasia of Lawrence's own partially understood unconscious. Lawrence draws the external, impersonal world inside him so he can express it again in personal, idiosyncratic fictions. Mr. Weiss follows him, wittily and scrupulously. This book is the most penetrating psychoanalytical inquiry into the latter-day Blake. It brings clarity to the Lawrentian darkness.

RICHARD ELLMANN

Evanston, Illinois
March, 1962

ACKNOWLEDGMENTS

I WISH to thank Professor Richard Ellmann of Northwestern University, whose good sense established the dimensions of this project; Professor Frederick Hoffman of the University of California at Riverside, whose own work, *Freudianism and the Literary Mind,* has become a landmark in Freudian criticism and whose suggestions have enriched this work; Naomi Pascal, whose good taste and eye for style have raised her editing on occasion to the level of coauthorship.

I am grateful to the Viking Press for permission to quote from the following titles published by them: *Sons and Lovers, A Modern Lover, The Prussian Officer, The Letters of D. H. Lawrence,* and *The Rainbow;* to the Hogarth Press for permission to quote from *The New Standard Edition of the Complete Psychological Works of Sigmund Freud;* to Jonathan Cape, Ltd., for permission to quote from E. T.'s *D. H. Lawrence: A Memoir;* to W. W. Norton and Company for permission to quote from Ernest Jones's *Hamlet and Oedipus.*

Passages from published articles in the *Northwest Review, Literature and Psychology* (the newsletter of the conference on literature and psychology of the Modern Language Association), and the *Northwestern Tri-Quarterly* appear in the present work.

I have introduced the art of the Expressionist painter, Edvard Munch (1863–1944), in these pages, impelled by the same sense of affinity that makes one connect Milton's *Paradise Lost* with Baroque architecture. Munch's subjects lend themselves to D. H. Lawrence's vision with a fidelity that is almost illustration.

I wish to thank J. H. Schultz Forlag in Copenhagen and Mr. Gunnar Stenersen of Forlaget Norsk Kunstreproduksjon for the privilege of using the pictures by Munch which grace this volume: "De ensomme" ("The Lonely Ones"), p. ii; "Omegas øyne" ("Omega's Eyes"), p. xii; "Mann og kvinne" ("Man and Woman"), p. 2; "Gravende arbeidere" ("Laborers"), p. 12; "Mannshode i kvinnehår" ("Man's Head in a Woman's Hair"), p. 38; "Vampyr" ("Vampire"), p. 68; "Harpy" ("Harpy"), p. 110.

D. A. W.

CONTENTS

OEDIPUS IN
NOTTINGHAM:
D. H. LAWRENCE

I

INTRODUCTION: THE PSYCHOANALYTIC COMMITMENT

WHAT MAKES the achievement of D. H. Lawrence so seductive to the modern reader is that, for all the strength of his successive philosophical positions, his work is marked more by emotional disruption than by finality. He proposes synthetic philosophies and esoteric psychological systems only to surrender them. He rightly considered that his books were, as he called them, "thought adventures." In making the attempt to explain the refractory aspects of Lawrence's art, I have been mindful that his total artistic evaluation depends on them. It is no use to speculate on what Lawrence might have been had he been furnished with a different outlook and a different set of ideas and passions. The impressive achievement not only of single books, but of his works as a whole, depends upon its mingling of the complex features of his mind. The challenge he proposes to respectable opinion, both literary and ethical, is as much a part of the fabric as the greatness, which even his detractors are more likely to affirm than deny.

So, in treating Lawrence's work, which is colored by the psychological discoveries of the twentieth century, I have found the works of the psychoanalytic school as essential for understanding the book as Lawrence's unconscious discovery of their materials was for writing it. Once the psychogenic origin of certain patterns of behavior in Lawrence's work is understood, some formulation in psychoanalytic terms is unavoidable.

The status of psychoanalytic criticism in the canon of respectable critical disciplines is no longer open to argument. But its origins as the love child of medical science and one of medicine's most original geniuses make its application to art seem merely a furthering of what medical science denounced to begin with as a miscegenation of disciplines. There seem to be two opposing feelings among those who consider psychoanalysis in relation to art. The first and simpler of these feelings is that a little bit of psychoanalysis goes a long way, and the other is that, if one is going to use just a little bit of psychoanalysis, he might just as well not use it at all. I do not sense in either camp, anti-Freudian or Freudian, the tendency to relax. Among the anti-Freudians, who condemn by omission, the feeling seems to be that if one gives in to psychoanalytic criticism none of their daughters, Emma, Jane Eyre, Becky Sharpe, or even Maisie, will be safe in her bed. The Freudians, on the other hand, confront themselves with what seems to be an imponderable problem—the transfer of the immense equipment of both theoretical and practical psychoanalysis on a professional basis into the field of criticism, without too clearly defined a notion of how it is to be applied.

Without presuming to number the hydra's heads, I should like to cite what I feel are some of the problems facing the future of psychoanalytic criticism.

The first I would call the problem of the amateur. Setting aside the embarrassment one must necessarily feel at using without a license the materials of a licensed profession, I mean by the amateur, the critic who renounces the practical purpose of psychoanalysis, which is after all not criticism but cure. Psychoanalysis in criticism, used undiluted, is an *aqua regia*; it effects no less than the reduction of literature to a limited number of preliterary elements, and the reduction of all human motives to their first cause in some primordial family situation. Thus, one is always a little uncomfortable when an analyst speaks about art: the inevitable note of patronage creeps in—as why should it not when the basic assumption is that the unconscious libido sleeps at its roots? His view of art makes of it a Palladian corridor of endless instances of the same act, a continuous sublimation or degradation of a limited number of eternal verities.

In capable hands, in Ella Sharpe's, for example, the tragedy of *King Lear* becomes a tragedy of bowel control, a phantasy from Shakespeare's anal period. The loose riotous knights, which Goneril and Regan deplore, are his feces, and his several daughters and sons-in-law represent aspects of the parent image. Such an analysis is comparable to Kenneth Burke's interpretation of *The Rime of the Ancient Mariner* as Coleridge's coming to terms with the monkey on his back. We are astounded by the skill displayed in either case, but we ask also, where has the poem gone? The discipline in each interpretation is not criticism but psychotherapy directed at the artist.

The consideration of a more or less esthetically perfect work at these depths has the unfortunate effect of yielding as its end product not the explicated work, but the protoplasmic material of its origin. One has thrown out the baby with the birth trauma.

Another unfortunate result of the too-professional analysis of the work of art is that the psychoanalytic critic has come to be regarded as an intellectual maggot whose proper meat is the diseased portions of whatever work he considers. This, the saprophytic function of psychoanalytic criticism, is the one to which Edmund Wilson lends his support in his metaphor of the "wound and the bow," the conviction that all art is by and large a cry of extraordinary pain. Lionel Trilling capably retorts in his essays, "Freud and Literature" and "Art and Neurosis," that the artist is not only *not* mentally ill but "possesses mental capabilities and psychic tone far superior to the normal man. . . . For, still granting that the poet is uniquely neurotic, what is surely not neurotic, what indeed suggests nothing but health, is his power of using his neuroticism. He shapes his fantasies, he gives them social form and reference."[1] In short, one must dissociate the creative act from the materials it deals with.

My feeling, then, is that psychoanalysis must be used with some caution, a caution more suited to the amateur than to the professional, in order, not to preserve the work of art, which is after all in no danger, but to preserve the critic who would peep and psychoanalyze upon his mother's grave from the temptation to ditch the esthetic altogether, and with it the concept of the work of art. I propose, in connection with literature, a lesser role for psychoanalytic criticism as a lay technique. From having been mildly interested in the psychological components of a work of art, the generality of readers is coming to insist that they be accurate, and inaccuracy puts as much of a tax on their sense of probability as gods from machines and other miraculous and melodramatic devices. The insistence arises from our having accepted, in the other, nonesthetic quadrants of our lives, certain psychological data as a guide to our understanding of ourselves. As individuals we are now psychologically interesting. Hamlet's Players, and their explicit play, "The Mouse Trap," are the outmoded external drama. The real dramatic interest has shifted to Hamlet. It is not that the Elizabethan mirror is shattered, but that the inner life is spectral and cannot see itself too clearly in a mirror. The psychological accuracy of an action is the new decorum.

T. S. Eliot punctiliously ignores this fact when he writes about *Hamlet:*

> The artistic "inevitability" lies in this complete adequacy of the external to the emotion; and this is precisely what is deficient in *Hamlet.* Hamlet (the man) is dominated by an emotion which is inexpressible, because it is in excess of the facts as they appear. And the supposed identity of Hamlet with his author is genuine to this point: that Hamlet's bafflement at the absence of objective equivalent to his feelings is a prolongation of the bafflement of his creator in the face of his artistic problem.[2]

Here Eliot is standing on the threshold of critical possibilities across which Freud had already walked.

> When [to quote from one of Freud's case histories] there is a mésalliance between an affect and its ideational content . . . a layman will say that the affect is too great for the occasion—that it is exaggerated—and that consequently the inference following . . . is false. On the contrary, the physician says: No. The affect is justified. . . . But it belongs to another content which is unknown (unconscious), and which requires to be looked for.[3]

To the extent that this "unknown" can be formulated and known through psychoanalytic method, artistic inevitability can be established (or re-established in those works of art which appear to be deficient in it). Hamlet's "excess of emotion" becomes "adequate" once the source of these affects is revealed. And the unformulated, feeling response of the spectator of the tragedy finds critical justification on a rational basis.

At its best, then, psychological criticism should constitute a bureau of tragic or comic weights and measures, testing in the work of art for the organic, psychologically valid material. If the material contains fortuities for the sake of some esthetic or formal purpose, then psychological criticism should betray the ersatz the way Solomon's bee betrayed Sheba's paper rose. Its amateur function should be analytic rather than reductive and therapeutic. It should recognize that the psychological background for a work of art constitutes, so to speak, its energy, but not its form, to which it is the parent.

In connection with the primacy of the work of art over its components another problem arises. It is the question (whose resolution implies radical differences in technique) of prototype or archetype, imago or archimago, under which king, Bezonian? Freud or Jung! Again the dilemma is confusing to the amateur. On the one hand Freudian criticism is full of grim warnings about attempting the interpretation of a work of art without closely integrated knowledge of the artist. Is psychoanalytic criticism essentially biography, acquired at first hand or hypothesized from the work? But if Freud makes too much of the specific provenance of the work of art, the Jungians, on the other hand, seem to ignore it completely in the grandiose structure of their psychology.

Jung at his best is a Freudian and a very good one. He serves also the good purpose of standing as a caveat to the Freudians against their tendency toward the provincial. Born out of the same psychological egg, Freud has contracted the human condition into a very dense, finite sphere of causes, while Jung has expanded the human psyche into a nebula stretching light years of thought back to the Magdalenians, even back to the protozoans. In their bearing toward literature the one suffers the cramp of meanness; the other, the vagueness of dispersion. At his worst the Freudian is a hairsplitter; the Jungian is a sleepwalker.

Assuredly the artist's life is of unique importance in the work of art. But, if we reject the notion that the etiology of the work lies always in some obscure hurt, or in some complex substitutive or restitutive process that is the exclusive peculiarity of one artist, then we can to a certain extent discount as critically unimportant the unknown or unknowable events in the artist's biography. And, if the worst comes to the worst, we can advance in the presumption that he *had* a life and that it was more or less like our own. What we have come to realize, with Freud, is that the standard, the commonplace experience in the artist's arsenal of available and valuable experiences is ultimately more important than the rare and the extraordinary experience.

As an example of such an experience and the attitude toward it that is almost absurdly typical of the modern sensibility, I should like to quote an excerpt from Volume I of Ernest Jones's *Life and Works of Sigmund Freud.* Jones is describing two of the most important events in Freud's early life. He writes:

> On the journey from Leipzig to Vienna a year later, Freud had occasion to see his mother naked: an awesome fact which forty years later he related in a letter to [Wilhelm] Fliess—but in Latin! . . .
>
> Darker problems arose when it dawned on him that some man was even more intimate with his mother than he was. Before he was two years old, for the second time another baby was on the way, and soon visibly so.
>
> Jealousy of the intruder, and anger for whoever had seduced his mother into such an unfaithful proceeding, were inevitable. Discarding his knowledge of the sleeping conditions in the house, he rejected the unbearable thought that the nefarious person could be his beloved and perfect father. It was early days to grapple with the inevitable problem of reality![4]

The tone is melodramatic, almost Dickensian; the material is utterly banal; the combination is mock-heroic. Yet, considering the edifice—or, for a moment to be cynical, the *industry*—this vision, seen through the eyes of genius, has raised, one must allow, the tone as completely fitted to the situation. It is compatible with the new decorum.

With an artist like Kafka it is almost essential that we consider domestic trifles before we attempt to come to any full understanding of his work. He does not seem to perform what was the time-honored function of the artist: to squeeze the universal into the local and finite dramatic situation—the tacit recognition of the correspondence between the macro- and the microcosm. Instead, he expands the local, the finite, in his case the family situation, into the universal. Kafka senior is not Our Father Which Art in Heaven, but Our Father Which Art in Heaven is Kafka the local haberdasher. In any but post-Freudian eyes this magnification might seem contemptible, the reduction absurd. But depth psychology has opened new vistas for the artist; and Kafka's vision has the validity of a coat described from inside out, in terms of seams, selvage, lining, and stains.

A further question remains of the artist's complicity in this psychoanalysis of art. To what extent is he conscious of his use of his insights into the depths? Is his work improved, damaged, or merely changed by the conscious use of psychoanalytic recognition? I feel that here the present need for psychological criticism is most justified. Stimulated by the fresh realities that have always lain like ancient cities beneath the naturalistic surface, the modern artist has set himself the task of exploring his unconscious. But he has not reckoned on the oxymoronic nature of darkness visible. It is not only Eros who vanishes when Psyche holds her candle to him; Psyche herself shrinks from illumination. The subject matter of the artist changes; the psychological energy and the disguises it wears maintain the same unconscious-conscious relationship. Sandor Ferenczi's description of the nature of symbol makes the relationship clear:

> Only such things (or ideas) are symbols in the sense of psychoanalysis as are invested in consciousness with a logically inexplicable and unfounded affect, and of which it may be analytically established that they owe this affective over-emphasis to *unconscious* identification with another thing (or idea), to which the surplus of affect really belongs. Not all similes, therefore, are symbols, but only those in which the one member of the equation is repressed into the unconscious. Rank and Sachs conceive a symbol in the same sense. "We

understand by this," they say, "a special kind of indirect representation . . . a substitutive, illustrative replacement-expression for something hidden."[5]

The writer, then, must pursue his unconscious bents in blindness, and the recognition of the psychological correctness of his work must of necessity be an a posteriori function of the critic. In fact the writer at this nonesthetic level of his activity cannot, should not win. His ignorance of the psychic process is no excuse to flout it. Indeed, it is more damning. And, on the other hand, any conscious tampering with the unconscious, like the attempts of some benighted Boeotian to give poor, dear Oedipus traveling directions to Thebes, merely makes the artist late for those marvelous appointments of his with Fate.

II

THE
FATHER
IN THE
BLOOD

IN THE sense, then, that psychoanalysis establishes artistic inevitability rationally where intuition has served or failed to serve, it is a valuable adjunct to the task of the formal critic. It has special applicability to the nondramatic genres, especially the novel, whose practitioners prefer the inscape of the mind because it is empirically more knowable than the "outward show" which "seldom or never jumpeth with the heart." In dealing with *Sons and Lovers*[1] as provocative of psychoanalytic investigation, I realize that I am proposing a paradox. Interpretation asks a mystery, and here there seems to be no mystery that the artist has not anticipated. Here *is* a contemporary Sophocles-Oedipus, armed with the knowledge, however scant, of the new depth psychology of Freud, creating unblinded a work of art out of the repressed materials of the unconscious. Lawrence appears to have made a dead set at the Oedipal relationship he experienced with his parents, sailing apparently into the winds that prevail against such a course. He seems even to have transferred, in an excess of literary cannibalism, characters still quick from the lives they lived with him, into the caldron of his art. And in his delineation of the relationship between Paul and his mother, from the beginning to their final recognition of the "something between them," there seems to be no holding back from the full orchestration of the primordial theme.

But, beneath Lawrence's conscious recognition and manifest working out of his Oedipal theme, psychoanalytic study reveals a latent, nocturnal reworking of the same theme, as if, as is so often true, the artist's unconscious had outrun his intention in a race to the same goal. In *Sons and Lovers* the artistic recognition of the material becomes itself a false recognition, a feint to catch the artist's eye while the real legerdemain of symbolic transformation does its work below the surface. In this subsurface we find unconscious material whose pertinence extends beyond the novel to include the remainder of his literary life—material from which spring the taut and devious relationships that distinguish Lawrence's protagonists. In short, *Sons and Lovers* is a coin whose reverse is the remainder of Lawrence's works. It contains as latencies those unborn attitudes to which the Lawrence who created Paul Morel seems a stranger.

Mark Schorer's essay, "Technique as Discovery," outlines the "discrepancies" in *Sons and Lovers* which "reveal certain confusions between intention and performance." The discrepancies are twofold: Lawrence failed to resolve his ambivalent feelings toward his parents—his identity with and his alienation from his father, his wish to be free of and his dependence on his mother; and he failed to come to artistic terms with the triad of women, Gertrude Morel, Miriam, and Clara. Of the second failure Schorer writes:

> The novel has two themes: the crippling effects of a mother's love on the emotional development of her son; and the split between kinds of love, physical and spiritual, which the son develops, the kinds represented by the two young women, Clara and Miriam. The two themes should of course work to-

gether, the second being actually the result of the first: this "split" is the "crippling." So one would expect to see the novel developed, and so Lawrence, in his famous letter to Edward Garnett where he says that Paul is left at the end with the "drift toward death," apparently thought he had developed it. Yet in the last few sentences of the novel, Paul rejects his desire for extinction and turns toward . . . life—as nothing in his previous history persuades us that he could unfalteringly do.[2]

The discrepancies Mark Schorer cites here cannot be explained away by any mechanical formulation of the process by which Paul Morel comes to the crossroads of his life. Lawrence himself offered such a formulation, summing up the intentional course of the novel in a sermonizing, portentous foreword meant, not for publication, but to satisfy an inner necessity of his own. The last page states the explicit purpose of *Sons and Lovers:*

> For in the flesh of the woman does God exact Himself. And out of the flesh of the woman does He demand: "Carry this of me forth to utterance." And if the man deny, or be too weak, then shall the woman find another man, of greater strength. And if, because of the Word, which is the Law, she do not find another man, nor he another woman, then shall they both be destroyed. For he, to get that rest and warmth, and nourishment which he should have had from her, his woman, must consume his own flesh, and destroy himself: whether with wine, or other kindling. And she, either her surplus shall wear away her flesh, in sickness, or in lighting up and illuminating old dead Words, or she shall spend it in fighting with her man to make him take her, or she shall turn to her son and say, "Be you my go-between."
>
> But the man who is the go-between from Woman to production is the lover of that woman. And if that Woman be his mother, then he is her lover in part only; he carries for her, but he is never received into her for his confirmation, and renewal, and so wastes himself away in the flesh. The old son-lover was Oedipus. The name of the new one is legion. And if the son-lover takes a wife, then she is not his wife, she is only his bed. And his life will be torn in twain, and his wife in her

despair shall hope for sons, that she may have her lover in her hour.[3]

The solution lies in ignoring such formulations as Lawrence has offered, and in focusing attention not on what Schorer calls "the self-righteous, aggressive, demanding mother" or the "simple, direct, gentle, downright fumbling ruined father," but upon the son and artist, whose double role is not that of the passive victim of these parental powers, but the very opposite—the only begetter of a wish-begotten drama in which he is the ultimate victor.

This study is guided by the conviction that the Oedipal situation, as Freud describes it, prevails in the novel. Moreover it prevails *against* Lawrence's attempts to direct it along enlightened lines, that is, as a drama in which the son does *not* obtain possession of the mother and does *not* seek his father's death. The novel contains, symbolically represented, a very real and physical rivalry between father and son for the same woman, and a very real defeat of the father; and, as a complement to this unresolved residue of guilt at defeating the father, an ensuing love and identification of the son with the father. The two themes, involving the mother and the two women, are not, as Mark Schorer states, unrelated as cause and effect, but have an essential role in the working out of the novel. And the end of the novel, Paul's choice of life, is a valid resolution of the ambivalences, the disruptive "psychological tension" which is the very substance of the novel.

In both Schorer's criticism and Lawrence's foreword there is a fundamental assumption whose acceptance obscures the essential action of the novel. *Sons and Lovers* (and Lawrence is clear enough on this point) is about the Oedipus complex. What Lawrence does not take into account (nor does his critic) is that the Oedipal situation is initiated by the son as his earliest attempt to establish himself in the family constellation. In his subjective consciousness parental influence is no more than an aggravating circumstance. Lawrence's instinctive reflex both in the novel and in his explanations of it has been to shift the burden of initiation, and of guilt, onto the shoulders of the parents. He has held the mirror up to nature and received an image reversed.

Jung's essay, "Symbolism of the Mother and Rebirth," describes the projection of guilt: "In order not to become conscious of his incest wish (this harking back to the animal nature), the son throws all the burden of guilt on the mother, from which arises the idea of the 'terrible mother.' The mother becomes for him a spectre of anxiety, a nightmare."[4]

Hamlet, as it exists as a psychological *aperçu* in the critical canon, sets the unnatural crime of incest far above the natural crime of murder, as being the more serious of the two. And on psychological criminal calendars Hamlet is the offender rather than Claudius, who is, if not nice, at least mature. Just as Laertes shifts the blame with his "The king, the king's to blame," so the desperately involved author-protagonist of *Sons and Lovers* cries, "The king *and* the queen are both to blame!" both in his introduction and in the consciously pursued action of the novel.

Without conjecturing upon the symbolic aptness of Gertrude Morel's Christian name, I believe that the action of *Hamlet* bears importantly on an understanding of *Sons and Lovers,* for the latter exhibits remarkable parallels to the play.

The most remarkable of these parallels underlies Walter Morel's role as the defeated father, and his subsequent roles as rival and idealized father image. I should like, first of all, to propose, tentatively, that Lawrence unconsciously rejected Walter Morel as Paul Morel's proper father, and, Hamlet-like, accepted him only as a despised stepfather. Certain internal evidence points to this. E. T. (Jessie Chambers), in her memoir of Lawrence, describes Lawrence's early draft of *Sons and Lovers,* in which she was somewhat disappointed:

> I could not help feeling that his treatment of the theme was far behind the reality in vividness and dramatic strength. Now and again he seemed to strike a curious, half-apologetic note bordering on the sentimental. . . . A non-conformist minister, whose sermons the mother helped to compose, was the *foil to the brutal husband* [italics mine].[5]

Here the phantasy of the idealized father has developed, as fortunately it has not in the novel. In *Sons and Lovers* the "nonconformist minister" shrinks to a reminiscence of John Field, the "son of a well-to-do tradesman," who "had been to college in London" and wanted to devote himself to the ministry. Circumstances separate them, and Gertrude meets and marries Walter Morel. Hyperion, as he is in *Hamlet,* has been buried, and the satyr rules in his place. The way lies open, as Ernest Jones suggests in his essay *Hamlet and Oedipus,* for the son to renounce his filial obligations of love and respect to someone who is merely a stepfather.

> In Hamlet the two contrasting elements of the normal ambivalent attitude toward the father were expressed toward two sets of people; the pious respect and love toward the memory of the father, and the hatred, contempt and rebellion toward the father substitutes, Claudius and Polonius. In other words, the original father has been transformed into two fathers, one good and the other bad, corresponding with the division in the son's feelings. With Caesar, on the other hand, the situation is simpler. He is still the original father, both loved and hated at once, even by his murderer.[6]

Freud offers a basis for such a phantasy in his essay "Family Romances." Originally, he says, a child wishes to be free from the authority of both parents equally. To realize this wish he rejects in phantasy his real parents in favor of idealized, dream parents, the kings and queens of the fairy tales. Later the phantasy is forced to a further modification. When the child realizes the true nature of the sexual relationship and "realizes that *pater semper incertus est* while the mother is *certissima*, the family romance undergoes a peculiar curtailment; it contents itself with exalting the child's father but no longer casts any doubts on his maternal origin."[7]

A second, more obviously parricidal phantasy, in which all rivals are done away with, both paternal and fraternal, is mentioned and correctly described in Harry Thornton Moore's life of Lawrence.

> Lawrence Clark Powell in the *Manuscripts of D. H. Lawrence* says that, in what is probably the earliest surviving holograph of *Paul Morel* [the original title of *Sons and Lovers*], the "father accidentally kills Paul's brother, is jailed, and dies upon his release." Once again, as in the first novel [summarized by E. T.], Lawrence was conveniently getting the father out of the way.[8]

In this situation the idealized unseen parent is overlooked, but the crime of murder relates the action to a Claudius-like father image.

Having conceived of an idealized father in the nonconformist minister of the first draft only to dismiss him, and having implicated the brutal father in a sordid murder in another version, Lawrence was then free to develop in Walter Morel the diapason of attributes that lay between these two, beginning first with his role as enemy and rival, and unworthy candidate for the hand of Paul Morel's mother.

The marriage of Gertrude Beardsall to Walter Morel is the marriage of a well-born lady to a miner whose origins are dubious. "His grandfather was a French refugee who had married an English barmaid—if it had been a marriage."[9] Here, to begin with, is the evolved family situation (to which actual events lend plausibility), in which the idealized father image has been read out of the work and so is, in effect, dead; and one has only the baseborn, inferior stepfather to deal with, the "bloat king" Claudius of *Hamlet*.

But intellectual and social inferiority are only the first step in the degradation of Walter Morel as the brutal stepfather. Just as for Hamlet sensuality and passion are personified in Claudius and are abhorred because, having identified his sexual objective with the king's, Hamlet feels guilty of a vicarious incest, so Lawrence's conception of Walter Morel gathers to itself a very special phallic imagery in which a little envy commingles with an immense disgust. The great *motif à rebours* of *Sons and Lovers* is the celebration of virginity, a celebration that Lawrence performs in many ways. E. T. records his reluctance to give up his childhood: "Lawrence was loath to admit that boyhood was over. He was most reluctant to begin shaving, and was hurt when people chaffed him about the pale hairs on his chin."[10] In a novel where to deflower is the crime, and the flower, to judge by the blossoms Lawrence scatters throughout the book, is preferred to the fruit, Walter Morel introduces always the undesirable phallic note into the scene.

In the very beginning of the novel there occurs a significant pair of offerings, one from Walter Morel, the other from Gertrude's son William. One is accepted, the other rejected. From the "wakes," the country fair, to which Gertrude Morel is hostile, William brings her a pair of egg cups decorated with moss roses. She accepts them. Later on Walter Morel returns, half drunk, and lays a coconut, "a hairy object," on the table. She does not thank him, merely shakes it to see if it has any milk, then "very tired, and sick of his babble, went to bed as quickly as possible, while he raked the fire."[11]

Even in his vocation Walter Morel, the miner, is a

creature of the underworld, the darkness. He compares himself to the "moudiwarp," the mole, a burrower in the earth. The imagery that envelops him is fleshy, red, moist, warm, nocturnal. In his first description of Walter, Lawrence deals kindly with him:

> He had wavy black hair that shone again and a vigorous black beard that had never been shaved. His cheeks were ruddy, and his red, moist mouth was noticeable because he laughed so often and so heartily . . . the dusky, golden softness of this man's sensuous flame of life that flowed off his flesh like the flame from a candle, not baffled and gripped into incandescence by thought and spirit. . . .[12]

This is Walter Morel—to pursue the phallic motif, tumescent—at a time before Paul's birth when the artist, describing the courtship between his parents, could afford to describe the idealized father, the nocturnal ruddy dancer. The successive incidents describe what may be called a progressive detumescence, a process accomplished, significantly enough, with the birth of Paul.

At first Morel is effective as the destroyer of flowers. William is his first victim when Morel cuts off his curls. The act is typical; on the surface an initiation into manhood of the son by the father, like Odysseus finding the overprotected Achilles among the women. But its effect, latent in the dream interpretation of haircutting, is symbolic castration:

> . . . the child, cropped like a sheep, with such an odd, round poll—looking wondering at her; and on a newspaper spread out upon the hearthrug, a myriad of crescent shaped curls, like the petals of a marigold scattered in the reddening firelight. . . . This act of masculine clumsiness was the spear through the side of her love for Morel.[13]

To the infantile observer, says Freud in his *Interpretation of Dreams*, sexual intercourse between parents appears to be an "act of violence and a fight." In *Sons and Lovers*, while the brief period of happiness between Walter Morel and Gertrude is unconvincingly touched upon, by far the most vivid descriptions of their relationship are those of Walter Morel's acts of violence against Gertrude. It is true that they take place in the lamplight of the kitchen, but the scenes are enveloped in a language that is full of the excessive loathing which is the attitude of the virginal adolescent toward his father, the disgust of the brothers Karamazov for old Karamazov.

It follows that the result of these "acts of violence" should be, from the son's point of view, in the phantasy of rivalry, the rejection of the father in favor of the son. Because it is to the son's advantage for the mother to remain virginal, saving herself for the son, Gertrude Morel in these scenes insulates herself in an imagery whose common property is purity, while Walter, in contrast, is swollen with blood.

> He came up to her, his red face, with its bloodshot eyes, thrust forward, and gripped her arms. She cried in fear of him, struggling to be free. Coming slightly to himself, panting, he pushed her roughly to the outer door, and thrust her forth, slotting the bolt behind her with a bang. Then he went back to the kitchen, dropped into his armchair, his head bursting, full of blood, sinking between his knees.
>
> The moon was high and magnificent in the August night. Mrs. Morel, seared with passion, shivered to find herself out there in a great white light, that fell cold in her, and gave a shock to her inflamed soul. . . . She became aware of something about her. With an effort she roused herself to see what it was that penetrated her consciousness. The tall white lilies were reeling in raw moonlight and the air was charged with their perfume, as with a presence.[14]

She is then pregnant with Paul. E. T. recalls that Mrs. Lawrence told her that Lawrence hated his father: "I know why he hates his father. It happened before he was born.

One night he put me out of the house. . . . He's bound to hate his father."[15]

After each one of these scenes of violence, Morel, defeated by Gertrude's purity, shrinks, detumesces. "Physically, even, he shrunk, and his fine, full presence waned. He never grew in the least stout, so that, as he sank from his erect, assertive bearing, his physique seemed to contract along with his pride and moral strength."[16]

The last violent scene between Paul Morel's parents culminates in a ceremony of blood, closing the circle around the son and his mother. Morel, in a rage, flings a drawer at Gertrude. It strikes her across the brow, wounding her. She keeps her consciousness, still holding the infant Paul in her arms. Morel is appalled at what he has done.

> He stood, bending forward, supported on his hands, which grasped his legs just above the knee. He peered to look at the wound. She drew away from the thrust of his face with its great moustache, averting her own face as much as possible. As he looked at her, who was cold and impassive as stone, with mouth tight shut, he sickened with feebleness and hopelessness of spirit. He was turning drearily away, when he saw a drop of blood fall from the averted wound into the baby's fragile, glistening hair. Fascinated, he watched the heavy, dark drop hang in the glistening cloud, and pull down the gossamer. Another drop fell. It would seep through into the baby's scalp. He watched, fascinated, feeling it soak in; then, finally, his manhood broke.[17]

The blood following the act of violence and Morel's subsequent decline are an unconscious reiteration of the identity between sex and violence and affirm the mother's fierce, unassailable virginity. Morel is bled out of the closing circle around mother and son. It is this deeper symbolism that gives real *ambiance* to the more consciously achieved effect of the mystic communion between Gertrude and Paul when her blood falls upon his head. Last of all it justifies itself artistically as a prophetic pantomime, a tragic irony. The blood of the mother is not on the father's head, but upon the son's.

Morel's phallic disintegration continues, under the critical eyes of his virginal rival. "There came over him [Morel] a look of meanness and paltriness. . . . Moreover Morel's manners got worse and worse, his habits somewhat disgusting."[18] And, while Morel's dissolution continues, the contrapuntal theme of Gertrude Morel's purity and fairy-tale nobility mounts in intensity. She is described as "queenly." She receives tribute from her sons "like a queen." "Mrs. Morel was one of those naturally exquisite people who can walk in mud without dirtying their shoes. But Paul had to clean them for her . . . and he cleaned them with as much reverence as if they had been flowers."[19] Out of this hyperbole, the queenliness of Gertrude, the bestiality of Walter, the devotion of the son, all of which represent the conscious rendering of the Oedipal theme by the artist, comes the final playing out of Walter Morel's role in the novel. But again it is to Shakespeare rather than to Sophocles one must turn for an analogous action.

Like Claudius, Morel guesses at the relationship between Gertrude and Paul. He walks in at a moment when Paul kisses her. " 'At your mischief again?' he said venomously." Angered, he throws Paul's supper into the fire. Paul leaps up to fight with him. They are about to come to blows when behind them they hear Gertrude moan in a faint. It is like the queen's slipping away in the midst of Hamlet's three-cornered duel. When she comes to herself again, Paul has only one concern. "Sleep with Annie, Mother, not with him." "No, I'll sleep in my own bed." "Don't sleep with him, Mother." "I'll sleep in my own bed."[20] Hamlet says:

> Refrain tonight
> And that shall lend a kind of easiness
> To the next abstinence: the next more easy [III. iv. 182–84].

Walter's recognition of the relationship between Paul and Gertrude accomplishes his destruction and more. He makes a continuation of the classical Oedipal theme on a manifest level impossible for the artist. Lawrence seems to have been acutely aware of the dilemma he created for himself. The strain begins to tell in the scene described above. The communion between the son and the mother becomes suddenly too intense:

> He had taken off his collar and tie, and rose, bare-throated, to go to bed. As he stooped to kiss his mother, she threw her arms round his neck, hid her face on his shoulder and cried, in a whimpering voice, so unlike her own that he writhed in agony.[21]

My concern here is not for Gertrude, but for the father, whose awareness of the secret makes his presence intolerable. It is my own belief that Lawrence suffered keenly for his exposure of the material touched upon in this passage, and that the passing of Morel from the novel as the effective father is the natural sequel to this exposure. Ernest Jones, discussing the infant phantasy and its repression in connection with *Hamlet*, touches upon "the complete expression of the 'repressed' wish . . . not only that the father should die, but that the son should then espouse the mother," as a "painful idea."[22] And it is the mother in both cases, in *Hamlet* because of the "infidelity" of Gertrude with Claudius, and in *Sons and Lovers* because of the nature of Gertrude's relationship with Paul, who brings to birth the repressed material. Of Hamlet's mother Jones says, "Her behaviour has stirred things in him that he cannot endure and which may make his life or his sanity impossible."[23]

It is significant that the chapters following this naked exploration of *leitmotif* are those which deal for the first time with Paul's sexual experiences with Clara and Miriam and his conflict with Clara's husband. What has happened?

The artist is still heavy with the obligation to pursue and resolve the Oedipal theme, in spite of its sudden transformation into an enormity. His strategy is traditional. He shifts the parental images from their bases in reality to the field of symbolic action. They become other people—in this case the "lovers." The "absence of family tie," as Jones explains Hamlet's almost casual murder of Polonius, releases Paul Morel from the narrow confines of a recognizable and dangerous relationship, allowing him to investigate in symbolically transformed terms those areas the "family tie" made inaccessible.

With the sentence that concludes the scene last described, "His last fight was fought in that home," the potency slips from Walter Morel in his role as a rival and transfers itself to Baxter Dawes, who is in *Sons and Lovers* a vitally important clue to the future development of the Lawrence protagonist. The superficial resemblance to Walter Morel can be dismissed in a few sentences. In physical appearance Baxter belongs to Morel's order of being: "white skin, with a clear, golden tinge," like Morel with his ruddy cheeks and moist, red mouth. He is also the rejected husband of a superior, sensitive woman. He works with his hands, a blacksmith, while his wife has educated herself beyond him. He becomes involved with Paul in a deadly rivalry for the same woman.

But the most revealing evidence that Walter Morel's paternal identity transfers itself to Baxter Dawes lies in Paul Morel's attitude toward Dawes. The psychoanalytic principle involved finds its clearest exposition in Freud's "Dostoevsky and Parricide."

Freud first of all discusses the ambivalent feeling of the son for his father. Combined with his hatred "a measure of tenderness is habitually present." Out of these combined attitudes comes a sense of identification with the father, a sense motivated not only by admiration but by a desire to supplant him. The progress of this twofold motivation is checked by a "powerful obstacle"—the fear of castration at the father's hands. In order to preserve his masculinity, the son relinquishes his wish to possess his mother and get rid of his father, but the survival of the wish in the unconscious forms the basis of a sense of guilt.

If, Freud continues, there is a strongly developed bisexuality in the child, then the threat to his masculinity may strengthen his inclination "to deflect in the direction of femininity, to put himself instead in his mother's place and take over her role as object of his father's love." But this alternative, because of the persistent fear of castration as the price of the father's love, is an equally impossible solution. And so both hatred and love of the father undergo repression.

Fear of the father makes hatred impossible, for it may be punished with castration. This direct fear of such punishment, and its concomitant of repressed hatred, Freud calls the normal factor in the Oedipus complex.

> Its pathogenic intensifications seem to come only with the addition of the second factor, the fear of the feminine attitude. Thus a strong innate bisexual predisposition becomes one of the preconditions, or reinforcements of neurosis. Such a predisposition must certainly be assumed in Dostoevsky, and it shows itself in a viable form (as latent homosexuality) in the important part played by male friendships in his life, in his strangely tender attitudes toward rivals in love, and his remarkable understandings of situations which are explicable only by repressed homosexuality, as many examples from his novels show. . . .
> If the father was hard, violent, and cruel, the super-ego [which Freud explains variously as cognate with conscience and as the permanent establishment in the ego of an identification with the father] takes over those attributes from him, and, in the relations between the ego and it, the passivity which was supposed to have been repressed is re-established. The super-ego has become sadistic, and the ego becomes masochistic, that is

to say, at bottom passive in a feminine way. A great need for punishment develops in the ego, which in part offers itself as a victim to fate, and in part finds satisfaction in ill-treatment by the super-ego.[24]

Similarly Ernest Jones touches upon the ambivalence with which the son regards the father:

> If, on the other hand, the "repression" of hostility is considerable, then the hostility toward the father will be correspondingly concealed from consciousness; this is often accompanied by the development of the opposite sentiment, namely an exaggerated regard and respect for him, and a morbid solicitude for his welfare, which completely cover the underlying relationship.[25]

The "tenderness," the compassion that tempers hatred, the "morbid solicitude," and the inclination to deflect in the direction of femininity are constants in the personality of the Lawrence protagonist. They are their purest in *Sons and Lovers*, because they are unconsciously rendered. There is no *raisonneur*, no Birkin of *Women in Love* or Lilly of *Aaron's Rod*, to justify the ways of a man with a man. Moreover, the line of descent, from father to friend to rival, is clearly traceable in the affinities between Walter Morel and Baxter Dawes.

Paul's preparation for his meeting with Dawes begins early, with the ambivalence in his feeling for his father:

> "Make him stop drinking," he prayed every night.
> "Lord, let my father die," he prayed very often.
> "Let him not be killed at pit," he prayed, when after tea the father did not come home from work.[26]

In the remissions from hatred of Walter Morel, Lawrence describes the compassion of Paul for his father, and even the pleasure Paul takes in his father's masculinity, as it expresses itself in his handiwork about the house and his life in the pits. But always the compassion is combined with a sense of separation and of fear, and later on, as Paul grows older, he looks through his mother's eyes with a tolerant contempt for his father's crotchets: "So she talked to her son, almost as if she were thinking aloud to him, and he took it in as best he could, by sharing her trouble to lighten it. And in the end she shared almost everything with him without knowing."[27] E. T. recalls this fine empathy between Lawrence and his mother: ". . . I heard him tell mother, in a voice that was clearly an unconscious imitation of his mother's, how Ernest and his fiancee had spent a fortnight's holiday with them, and that it had proved something of a strain."[28]

Reserving a fuller discussion of Clara Dawes for later, I cannot omit touching upon her now in connection with Baxter Dawes and Paul Morel. For Baxter and Clara are the new parental constellation in the novel, the foster parents, devoid of "family tie," with whom Paul will act out the repressions that obscure his relations with Walter and Gertrude. It is his interest in Clara that quickens his interest in Dawes, and his interest in her is heightened by his curiosity about her marriage to Dawes and her subsequent "revulsions" from him. Following Paul's frustrated attempts to come to terms with Miriam, he fixes upon Clara. It is through her that he first satisfies his curiosity about Dawes. His interrogation of her is significant. As the interrogator Paul seems to be working out a new solution more feasible than the one awaiting him at home. He asks questions about a rival of whom he has foreknowledge:

"You went to sleep as you grew to be a woman? How queer! And he didn't wake you?"

"No; he never got there," she replied in a monotone.

The brown birds dashed over the hedges where the rose-hips stood naked and scarlet.

"Got where?" he asked.

"At me. He never really mattered to me."[29]

Everything, even the floral commentary, the sudden flurry

of brown birds among the rose-hips, is a reflection of Paul's prophetic soul and his triumph over the older man.

But after this triumph the sense of guilt comes again, and with it the "morbid solicitude," as Jones describes it. Paul becomes the devil's advocate. Clara describes Baxter's brutality, and Paul defends him:

> "But did you—were you ever—did you ever give him a chance?"
> "Chance? How?"
> "To come near to you."
> "I married him—and I was willing."—
> They both strove to keep their voices steady.
> "I believe he loves you," he said.
> "It looks like it," she replied.[30]

The thrusting of Baxter upon an unwilling Clara is a reflection of Paul's unwillingness, in spite of his very real physical attraction toward her, to pursue what must appear, latent in Lawrence's handling of the subject, as an unnatural offense against the older man. The triumph implicit in Dawes's "never getting there," and the *noblesse oblige* toward a rival too much like one's self, act as spur and rein and frustrate Paul: "He was like so many young men of his own age. Sex had become so complicated in him that he would have denied that he ever could want Clara or Miriam or any woman whom he *knew*. Sex desire was a sort of detached thing, that did not belong to a woman."[31]

In every encounter with Dawes, Paul's ambivalence toward him reveals itself:

> Paul and he were confirmed enemies, and yet there was between them that peculiar feeling of intimacy, as if they were secretly near to each other, which sometimes exists between two people although they never speak to each other. Paul often thought of Baxter Dawes, often wanted *to get at him* and be friends with him. He knew that Dawes often thought about him, and the man was drawn to him by some bond or other.

And yet the two never looked at each other save in hostility [italics mine].[32]

The same tenderness pervades a scene of open conflict with Dawes. The older man insults Paul, who dashes a glass of wine in his face.

He hated Dawes, wished something would exterminate him at that minute; and at the same time, seeing the wet hair on the man's forehead, he thought that he looked pathetic. He did not move . . . Paul had a curious sensation of pity, almost of affection mingled with violent hate for the man.[33]

When Paul tells Clara about the incident and she is furious with Dawes, Paul defends him to her:

"Yet you married him," he said. . . .
"I did!" she cried, "but how was I to know?"
"I think he might have been rather nice," he said.[34]

This Christ-like forbearance is suspect; it is not the "detached criticism" of the cool intellect that Lawrence says it is. The "thrusting forward" of Dawes's "handsome, furious face" is a reminder of the thrusting forward of another furious face that simultaneously demanded and denied his love. The ego, which Freud describes as "offering itself as a victim to fate," demands a passivity from Paul, and even a desire to be a victim. He refuses, when Clara urges him to protect himself from Baxter, to take any defensive measures. To her "And if he kills you?" his reply is, "I should be sorry for his sake and mine."

Paul's opportunity to submit is offered to him by Dawes in their battle together. It is a test of Paul, and his behavior in the fight, and its outcome, gather together both the unconscious conflicts and their symbolic realization to a point of fusion. All of Lawrence's physical struggles between men are the wrestling of Jacob with the angel at the ford, ending in apocalyptic revelation. With Dawes's life in his hands, Paul recognizes his adversary and the nature of the crime.

Even in describing the struggle the language ventures beyond violence:

> Pure instinct brought his hands to the man's neck, and before Dawes, in frenzy and agony, could wrench him free, he had got his fingers twisted in the scarf and his knuckles dug in the throat of the other man. He was a pure instinct without reason or feeling. His body, hard and wonderful, in itself, cleaved against the struggling body of the other man; not a muscle in him relaxed. He was quite unconscious, only his body had taken upon itself to kill this other man. . . . Then suddenly he relaxed, full of wonder and misgiving.[35]

At the last Paul reverts, offering himself "as a victim to fate." Dawes, released, kicks him into unconsciousness and leaves him.

In the outcome of the fight, when Paul, with the other man's life in his hands, relents and is finally defeated by Dawes, Lawrence has defined the interior conflict in his protagonist's mind. Like David (a favorite of Lawrence), who spares Saul's life but cuts off the hem of his garment, Paul commits just the right degree of parricide, recoils, and offers himself in atonement for the crime.

His first thought, when he recovers consciousness, is to get back to his mother. "That was his blind intention." Gertrude Morel sits by his bedside, distraught. "There was something between them that neither dared mention. Clara came to see him. Afterward he said to his mother: 'She makes me tired, mother.' "[36] It is the sense of having ventured too far, of being allowed to venture too far, in a relationship sanctioned by conventional society, and into a hostility that has finally no admixture of compassion, that drives Paul back upon his mother. Here, at least, the "something between them" need never be explored, and his conflict with his father, while actual enough, had ended without overt physical violence. The return to Gertrude is a return from the rigors of reality. The irony consists of his being driven back into the unspeakable Oedipal situation through his recognition of that situation in what should have been a more acceptable surrogate for it—the rivalry with an older man for the possession of his wife.

That Dawes's attack on Paul ultimately ends in Paul's physical defeat does not contradict the psychological truth of the action, in which Dawes is morally defeated by the same symptomatic "morbid solicitude" that characterizes Paul's attitude toward him. Paul goes to visit Dawes at the hospital.

> There was a feeling of connexion between the rival men, more than ever since they had fought. In a way Morel felt guilty toward the other, and more or less responsible. And being in such a state of soul himself, he felt an almost painful nearness to Dawes. . . . Besides they had met in naked extremity of hate, and it was a bond. At any rate the elemental man in each had met.[37]

Paul's return to his mother as a helpless, beaten child is his effective, but costly, unconscious solution of his problem. His helplessness is a regression to a childhood whose epicene (castrate) nature would allow him possession of his mother without further fear of his father. And in this regressive action is implicit his rejection of Clara. Unsexed, he no longer has need of her.

In his further gesture, the return of Clara to Dawes, Paul extends the regressive nature of his act to include the closing of the parental arch over his head again—an arch that in his own real family is crumbling. He strives to commit the ultimate in self-abnegation, the martyrization, as Freud suggests, of the ego by the stern parental superego. In the process Dawes is elevated to the level of the idealized father:

> But Dawes now carried himself quietly, seemed to yield himself, while Paul seemed to screw himself up. Clara thought she had never seen him look so small and mean. He was as if

> trying to get himself into the smallest possible compass. . . .
> Watching him unknown she said to herself there was no
> stability in him. He was fine in his way, passionate, and able to
> give her drinks of pure life when he was in one mood. And now
> he looked paltry and insignificant. There was nothing stable
> about him. Her husband had more manly dignity. . . . And
> yet she watched him rather than Dawes, and it seemed as if
> their three fates lay in his hands.[38]

Paul has now become "paltry and insignificant," in the terms
he uses to describe Walter Morel earlier in the book, and
restores Baxter Dawes to Clara. But in exchange for these
sacrifices their "three fates lay in his hands." He has become,
in this re-creation of the family, the idealized son, who
through suffering and sacrifice has achieved knowledge and
power, the attributes of messiah-hood, an acceptance through
expiation.

There is an unconscious causality between the fight with
Dawes, the death of Paul's mother, and the return, after her
death, of Clara to Dawes—a causality that finds its source
in Paul's fight with his father. As, earlier in the novel, he
and Walter glare at each other prepared to strike, Gertrude
faints away. It is as if in the actual conflict she recognized
herself as the prize. The result of this first conflict was also
a revelation, a subrational "recognition" on the part of the
father, and a recoil on the part of the artist, that sent his
protagonist adventuring among strangers. After the fight
with Dawes, Gertrude Morel "faints" again, but this time
the disease is mortal. For Paul, whose vague, shifting burden
of guilt could attach a ritual significance to his battle with
Dawes, his open conflict with the man for his wife has
brought about his mother's death. With his mother dead,
and his father reduced to ineffectuality, Paul's feelings of
guilt and "responsibility" are transferred to Clara and Dawes.
In giving her back to Dawes, he says in effect, "I took you
from my father with disastrous results. Now I give you back

to avoid making the same mistake." Dawes becomes the idealized father image; Clara, the assessor. And Paul's act of Christ-like renunciation and expiation is, like Dostoevsky's acceptance of the Little Father of Mother Russia, a repression of his hostility against his father, an acceptance, an idealization, and finally an identification.

Paul's undertaking to rescue Dawes from his despondency is in these terms the resolution of the impulse to be quits with the father, to return good for evil. Freud's general description of such a restitutive act, contingent upon certain other conditions, also present in the novel, urges this interpretation of the younger man's actions. A man in the throes of an unresolved Oedipus complex will often choose as his love object a woman who is essentially a mother surrogate. He will synthesize the family situation by making her the possession, preferably legal, of another man. She will also, because we are dealing here with sexual maturity, be sexually available. Freud suggests that certain independent aspects of the original family situation are carried over into this relationship, and one of these is being quits with the father through some special act of kindness to him:

> In actual fact the "rescue-motif" has a meaning and history of its own, and is an independent derivative of the mother-complex, or more correctly of the parental complex. When a child hears that he *owes his life* to his parents or that his mother *gave him life*, his feelings of tenderness unite with impulses which strive at power and independence, and they generate the wish to return this gift to the parents and to repay them with one of equal value. It is as though the boy's defiance were to make him say: "I want nothing from my father. I will give him back all I have cost him." He then forms the phantasy of *rescuing his father from danger and saving his life*; in this way he puts his accounts square with him.[39]

To Freud's note on the "rescue" of the man as a corollary to the rescue of the woman, Karl Abraham adds another component that may serve to explain the necessity behind the failure of Paul and his father to come to actual blows, and to explain also, even more fully than Freud, the repetition of these violent encounters, culminating in at least one fatality, in others of Lawrence's stories. It is a more sinister component than the one Freud suggests; it is that the original phantasy is the very opposite of rescue, is in fact attack and murder, and that it undergoes repression and is transferred into its opposite. In his clinical work Abraham encountered regularly in some of his male patients phantasies involving rescuing their fathers from runaway horse-drawn carriages. Beneath this apparent solicitude lay always the repressed wish to remove the father in another sense, equating the galloping horses less with danger than with a sexual union with the mother, and the removal of the father with a death wish.

Returning to the original Oedipus myth, Abraham observed the similarity in the physical encounter between Oedipus and Laius, except that here there is no rescue. But, as Abraham points out, another form of disguise occurs. The son's slaying of the father is deflected to a safely arranged tale of a struggle between strangers. The repression of the original phantasy is thus only partial, and the parricidal content of the phantasy is allowed full sway.

> It is significant that the father first uses force against the son, whereupon the son replies with a blow, which, however, *he does not direct against the father himself*, but against the driver, that is to say, a substitute for the father. Then the father attacks the son, and it is only at the end, and as an act of self-defense, that the son kills him. Here the same sequence occurs at the beginning of the myth. The father threatens the life of the newly-born son, so that the later deed of Oedipus bears the character of retaliation, and is thus to some extent mitigated.
>
> . . . In the rescue-phantasy these wishes have been made more recognizable than in the myth with which it has been compared; this has been brought about by means of repression

and distortion, involving the turning of these wishes into their opposite [italics mine].[40]

If we recollect the scenes of violence Lawrence describes as having taken place in Paul's infancy, culminating in the narrowly averted fight with his father in his youth, we can see in Paul's fight with Dawes a corollary to the blows Oedipus deflected to the drivers of his father's carriage. The primordial death wish emerges into overt action only with a substitute for the father. Dawes takes the brunt of the withheld blow. He is only a "driver."

But even here the son lapses into the dreamlike incompletion of the act, and the more dominant rescue phantasy commands again.

The return of Clara to Dawes is also in the nature of a "rescue," the saving of Clara from a moral fall that Paul himself has brought about. In effect it is a restoration of the mother to her former purity, and with it the achievement of a state of rest, a truce that will perfect itself through the rest of Lawrence's work, between himself and the father.

III

THE
MOTHER
IN THE
MIND

GERTRUDE MOREL moves through *Sons and Lovers* like a cry of pain. Her truth is valid only as she is an expression of her son's anguish—and this both in spite of and because of the clinical verisimilitude with which Lawrence images her as the Jocasta par excellence. Of the other characters it can be said that Lawrence is truly their creator, since they live in obedience to their own laws. But of Gertrude Morel he is merely the undertaker, responsible for her careful embalming. Her likeness is a magnificent death mask. Around her cluster the metaphors of queenliness, and virginity, and youth, the mechanically collated evidence of the Oedipal relationship. Her son William was "like her knight who wore *her* favor in the battle." When she goes into town with Paul, they feel "the excitement of lovers having an adventure together." "She was gay like a sweetheart. . . . As he saw her hands in their old black gloves getting the silver out of the worn purse, his heart contracted with pain of love for her."[1]

The inevitable wish of the child that his mother remain young becomes the conscious theme of Paul's outbursts:

> "Why can't a man have a *young* mother? What is she old for? . . . And why wasn't I the oldest son? Look—they say the young ones have the advantage—but look, *they* had the young mother. You should have had me for your eldest son."
>
> "I didn't arrange it," she remonstrated. "Come to consider, you're as much to blame as me." He turned on her, white, his eyes furious.[2]

Here the subtle disguise Paul's wish wears is the important thing. His real desire is to be even more than the "oldest son," is not even that his mother remain young, but that they be equal in age no matter what it is.

Lawrence completely idealizes Gertrude's maternal role as the mother of the infant Paul. She is Rachel, the virginal mother.

> Mrs. Morel watched the sun sink from the glistening sky, leaving a soft, flower-blue overhead. . . . A few shocks of corn in a corner of the fallow stood up as if alive; she imagined them bowing; perhaps her son would be a Joseph. In the east a mirrored sunset floated pink opposite the west's scarlet. The big haystacks on the hillside that butted into the glare went cold.
>
> In her arms lay the delicate baby. . . . She no longer loved her husband. She had not wanted this child to come, and there it lay in her arms and pulled at her heart. . . . She would make up for having brought it into the world unloved. She would love it all the more now it was here; carry it in her love.[3]

Gertrude's virginal quality expresses itself chiefly in floral arrangements. She soothes herself with "the scent of flowers"; she is Flora, never Ceres, having long ago chosen between her son's moss rose and Walter Morel's unhappy, hairy coconut.

The necessity for this purity rests, not with Gertrude, but with Paul. It is his wish that she remain pure. Freud suggests that "the grown man's conscious mind likes to regard the mother as the personification of impeccable moral purity"[4] out of an unconscious jealousy of the father and a horror of adult sexuality. And E. T., writing of Lawrence's disgust at hearing "commercial travellers" talking on a train, remembers "that the whole question of sex had for him the fascination of horror, and also that in his repudiation of any possibility of a sex relation between us he felt that he paid me a deep and subtle compliment."[5] The nature of the compliment will be taken up in connection with a discussion of Miriam.

Yet through the mask of Lawrence's mother there emerge occasionally the living signs of the deathly relationship between Paul and Gertrude Morel. Gertrude's careful distinction between the mind and the body, made originally in her relations with William when she refuses to acknowledge his manhood and its needs, leads, in her life with Paul, to a love affair of the spirit. And with Paul she is freer to lead it, for it is with his complicity. When Paul's picture wins a prize at the Castle, Mrs. Morel cries, "Hurrah my boy! I knew we should do it!" as if it were a child they had borne between them.

Confronted with Paul's mistresses she directs most of her bitterness against the one who most resembles herself, Miriam, the one whom Paul likewise recognizes as his mother's rival. Her judgments of Miriam are true for both of them: " 'She is one of those who will want to suck a man's soul out till he has none of his own left,' she said to herself; 'and he is just such a baby as to let himself be absorbed. She will never let him become a man; she never will.' "[6]

In the scene leading up to the discovery by Walter Morel of Paul and Gertrude embracing, that point after which, I have suggested, the real nature of the relationship becomes intolerable, Paul, Miriam, and Gertrude are involved in almost a fairy-tale situation. Paul is tending his mother's bread, setting the loaves to bake. Miriam is there, and a hoydenish, sensual girl named Beatrice. It is Beatrice who teases him and plays with him sexually, and Miriam, prudish and as disapproving as his mother would have been, who reminds him that the loaves are burning. Quickly he takes the loaf from the oven, scrapes it, and sets it aside. When he returns from having seen Miriam home, he finds his mother, pale and blue-lipped with the beginnings of her illness, the charred loaf on the table in front of her. "I suppose it's my heart,"[7] is her explanation of her illness, but her mental concern is that she supposes Paul to have been too engrossed in Miriam to mind the loaf. And the loaf itself, like the giant's egg in the fairy tale, becomes the external repository of Gertrude's heart.

The little story seems to contain within it the irony of identities failing to recognize one another. Mrs. Morel does not realize that it is not through Miriam that her grasp on Paul will be destroyed, but through the more wholesome sensuality of a Beatrice. When we consider Clara Dawes we find Lawrence attributing to Gertrude a preference for her rather than for Miriam. It is the expression of a wish whose fulfillment would preserve the spiritual nexus in which Paul and Gertrude meet as lovers. The addition of Clara (who, as we shall see, did not exist but had to be invented) to the relationship would provide a *modus vivendi* for both mother and son. Gertrude is made to see this:

> Mrs. Morel considered. She would have been glad now for her son to fall in love with some woman who would—she did not know what. But he fretted so, got so furious suddenly, and again was melancholic. She wished he knew some nice woman —She did not know what she wished, but left it vague.[8]

For Clara represents the dancing side of the relationship, which neither she nor Miriam could provide. And both Gertrude and Miriam give Clara to him in order to purge his spiritual nature of its fleshly dress and to have him back refined and virginal. But it is important to remember that it is Paul who is the unconscious seeker, and the one, ultimately, who realizes the need Clara can satisfy in him.

Mrs. Morel's compliance with the idea of Clara is the compliance of a woman putting her child out to wet-nurse. For Paul the sexuality Clara offers is feasible incest, just as his relationship with Miriam, although consummated, is not; and both relationships are determined by the root Oedipal relationship.

The death of Lawrence's mother came about as the result of natural causes; the death of Mrs. Morel has the tragic inevitability of Clytemnestra's murder or Jocasta's suicide. It is the sequel to revelation, which presents two equally horrid alternatives to the protagonist: either the conscious continuation of an unnatural relationship, or the cessation by death of any such possibility. I have suggested that the artist of *Sons and Lovers* brought the passional side of his affair with his mother to a halt when it threatened to become an enormity. Symptomatic of that enormity were the recognition by the father of the "mischief" Paul and his mother were up to and the subsequent beginnings of a real physical struggle between father and son. It is the mother's fainting, not her death but the simulacral prefiguring of her death, that brings about Paul's search in the ensuing chapters of the novel for a mother substitute, if not a way out completely. The enfeebling of Gertrude puts her beyond being desirable as a sexual object, the girl who could race up a hill and who attracted Walter Morel. More and more, fuller and deeper complexities of "terror, agony, and love" are injected into the descriptions of Paul's love for his mother: "His life wanted to free itself of her. It was like a circle where life turned back on itself, and got no further."[9] It is at this point that he is sexually involved, for the first time with some success, with Clara, the younger rival in a new triangle. His open, terrible, revealing fight with Baxter Dawes is followed, as his narrowly avoided fight with Walter Morel is followed, by another failure in Gertrude's health, this time a fatal one.

The recognition, as Lawrence consciously indicates it, is

now complete. And his task, as before, is to render its consummation impossible. Now, in accord with the old myth, following the parricide and the achieved marriage (with both Clara and Miriam), the mother must be destroyed. "He and his mother seemed almost to avoid each other. There was some secret between them which they could not bear. He was not aware of it. He only knew that his life seemed unbalanced, as if it were going to smash into pieces."[10] Gertrude's cancer comes as a relief to this stalemate, like the diabolical fulfillment of an oracle. For at the heart of Paul's anguish lies an unconscious awareness of the secondary advantage to be gained from her death—she will be preserved to him. One of his great wishes has been that she remain young and uncorrupted, virginal. As the terminator of life, death is also the preserver of life, a bitter truism that suicides must intuitively grasp, pinching their lives off to anticipate destruction. Gertrude, dying, gathers to herself the imagery of youth:

> He sat down by the bed, miserably. She had a way of curling and lying on her side, like a child. The grey and brown hair was loose over her ear.
> "Doesn't it tickle you?" he said, gently putting it back.
> "It does," she replied.
> His face was near hers. Her blue eyes smiled straight into his, like a girl's—warm, laughing with tender love. It made him pant with terror, agony, and love.[11]

And with her death the transformation is complete. She becomes the fulfillment of his wish: "She lay like a maiden asleep. With his candle in his hand, he bent over her. She lay like a girl asleep and dreaming of her love. . . . She was young again. . . . She would wake up. She would lift her eyelids. She was with him still."[12]

Paul's other great wish is that he himself may die. When Lawrence writes about Paul, his artistic ego, he continually offers himself, like Dostoevsky, "as a victim to fate." The flow of pity between Gertrude and Paul is continually being reciprocated, each one anguished at the other's doomed quality, each one guilty because he cannot alter fate.

> She listened to the small, restless noise the boy made in his throat as she worked. Again rose in her heart the old, almost weary feeling towards him. She had never expected him to live. And yet he had a great vitality in his young body. Perhaps it would have been a little relief to her if he had died. She always felt a mixture of anguish in her love for him.[13]

Gertrude's anguish is related to her thought of the "relief" it might have brought her if Paul had died, and similarly Paul's anguish and wish to die find their source in his open hostility and death wish toward his father, and in his repressed death wish toward his mother when her love threatens his manhood.

Gertrude's death gives rise in Paul to a very dangerous line of thought: that in dying he will be with his mother, just as the minister promises Gertrude that she will be with her son William. "Sometimes they looked into each other's eyes. Then they almost seemed to make an agreement. It was almost as if he were agreeing to die also."[14] Paul waters her milk to weaken her, and finally he administers an overdose of morphia to her—all as if he were sending her ahead to an assignation.

> "What are you doing?" said Annie.
> "I s'll put 'em in her night milk."
> Then they both laughed together like two conspiring children. On top of all their horror flickered this little sanity.[15]

What gives the death of Gertrude its special intensity and importance—Paul's reaction to it is the point on which the novel resolves itself—is the unwritten confusion in the artist's mind. Gertrude's death is at once a real death and a sexual death. Never is she described with such amorous concern as when she is on her deathbed, dreaming her young dream. She is, for the first time in the novel, sexually desirable and seemingly available to the son. His only rival skulks below stairs and will not even look at her. Walter Morel is afraid of her. Only Paul is her lover. "They all stood back. He kneeled down and put his face to hers and his arms round her: 'My love—my love—oh, my love!' he whispered again and again. 'My love—oh, my love.' "[16] But the agent that brings about both these deaths, Death itself, is Fate, God, the father in his destructive phase. Paul's speeding of Gertrude's death is simply one more attempt to interpose himself between his father and his mother. Even when she first becomes sick, his attempt to save her is halfhearted. He knows she must die.

And finally, when he kisses her "passionately" and feels a "coldness against his mouth," he is brought to a last realization and choice. Like Baxter with Clara, he cannot get "at her." He must, as he does with Baxter Dawes, return her to the father, or else, in a continuation to the end of the closed circle, follow his mother into death for the sake of her embrace. William, Paul's brother, of whom he was "unconsciously jealous," faced the same choice earlier in the novel. Preoccupied, like Paul, with death, he anticipates his mother and prepares a place in the grave before her. Like Gertrude's death, William's death *really* happened to Lawrence's brother Ernest; what is more important, as in Gertrude's death, is that William's death *must* happen in *Sons and Lovers* to justify William's part in the novel. William's is the way not taken, the negation of Paul's choice. William's way is consciously rejected, at the end of the novel, by Paul: " 'Mater, my dear—' he began, with the whole force of his soul. Then he stopped. He would not say it. He would not admit that he wanted to die, to have done. He would not own that life had beaten him, or that death had beaten him."[17]

So far we have traced the father image from an idealized figure in the prehistory of *Sons and Lovers* through Walter Morel, ending finally in some resolution of conflict between

Paul and Baxter Dawes. We have observed that the initial family situation, under repression, transferred itself to a triangle in which Dawes and Clara reiterated the parental scheme. And finally we have investigated in Gertrude Morel those areas which overemphasis of her Sophoclean role has partially occulted. It remains to trace her influence upon Paul's other women, Miriam Leivers and Clara Dawes, to examine the Freudian determinants of the parts they play in *Sons and Lovers*.

Freud postulates the unconscious "conditions of love" that govern the objects of the affections of certain men. The more urgent of these conditions Freud terms "the need for an injured third party," that is, the Oedipal man's choice of woman will require that she be attached to someone else, lover or husband, who has some "right of possession" over her. The second condition, operating as a corollary to the first, requires that the woman be in some way "sexually discredited," the subject of gossip, "loose," or openly promiscuous. With the fulfillment of these conditions the lover conceives of his role as being that of rescuer, rescuing the woman he loves from moral, economic, or social ruin.[18]

The etiology of these strange patterns of choice and response, says Freud, is identical with the normal pattern of love:

> They are derived from the infantile fixation of tender feelings on the mother, and represent one of the consequences of that fixation. In normal love, only a few characteristics survive, which reveal unmistakably the maternal prototype of the object-choice; as, for instance, the preference shown by young men for mature women; the detachment of libido from the mother has been effected relatively swiftly. In our type, on the other hand, the libido has remained attached to the mother for so long, even after the onset of puberty, that the maternal characteristics remain in the love-objects that are chosen later, and all these turn into easily recognizable mother-surrogates.[19]

The "injured third party" is immediately recognizable as the father, in the family situation as the child first conceives of it, with the mother as the sole object of his love. The choice of the "loose" woman seems at first paradoxical, since men tend normally to think of their mothers as being morally impeccable. But the preference derives from the unstable amalgam the son must construct from things as he wants them and things as they are. His first response, upon learning about adult sexuality, is to deny his mother's complicity in such an act. And then, when he can no longer cling to the logical absurdity of such a denial, he swings with a "cynical logic" to the identification of his mother with any sexually available woman:

> The enlightening information he has received has in fact awakened the memory-traces of the impressions and wishes of his early infancy, and these have led to a reactivation in him of certain mental impulses. He begins to desire the mother herself in the sense with which he has recently become acquainted, and to hate his father anew as a rival who stands in the way of his wish; he comes, as we say, under the dominance of the Oedipus complex. He does not forgive his mother for having granted the favours of sexual intercourse not to himself but to his father, and he regards it as an act of unfaithfulness. . . . As a result of the constant, combined operation of the two driving forces, desire and thirst for revenge, phantasies of the mother's unfaithfulness are by far the most preferred; the lover with whom she commits her act of infidelity almost always exhibits the features of the boy's own ego, or more accurately, of his own idealized personality, grown up and so raised to a level with his father.[20]

Ernest Jones refers to a similar deviation in object choice when he discusses Hamlet's sexual revulsion, his cruel abuse of Ophelia, and his "complex reaction" toward his mother:

> The underlying theme relates ultimately to the splitting of the mother image which the infantile consciousness effects into two opposite pictures: one of the virginal madonna, an in-

accessible saint towards whom all sensual approaches are unthinkable, and the other of a sensual creature accessible to everyone. . . .

When sexual repression is highly pronounced, as with Hamlet, then both types of women are found to be hostile: the pure one out of resentment at her repulses, the sensual one out of the temptation she offers to plunge into guiltiness. Misogyny, as in the play, is the result.[21]

Miriam's contribution to the composite mother image is her purity. She is the "virginal madonna," the "virtuous and reputable woman," the "personification of impeccable moral purity," that aspect of the mother image that represents the spiritual, the physically untouchable. Like Gertrude she prefers the blossom to the fruit. On their first visit to the Spinney Farm, Paul and Gertrude are in "ecstasy together" over the gillivers and guelder roses, bluebells and forget-me-nots, a pleasure Miriam shares with them. It is her coarse brothers who tell Paul that if he picks the apple blossom there will be no apple, and who tease Miriam for not being able to stand the sharp peck the hen makes at the corn in her hand. She is afraid of Paul's painting of pine trees towering in a red sunset. "Paul took his pitch from her and their intimacy went on in an utterly blanched and chaste fashion. It never could be mentioned that the mare was in foal."[22]

Upon Miriam, Lawrence heaps even more extravagant attributes of purity than upon Gertrude Morel, who has in some degree "fallen" through her marriage a victim to sexuality. Miriam is a *religieuse*:

And she was cut off from ordinary life by her religious intensity which made the world for her either a nunnery garden or a paradise where sin and knowledge were not, or else an ugly cruel thing.[23]

All the life of Miriam's body was in her eyes, which were usually dark as a dark church, but could flame with light like a conflagration. . . . She might be one of the women who went with Mary when Jesus was dead. . . . There was no looseness or abandon about her.[24]

Her resemblance to Ophelia approaches paraphrase. Paul writes to Miriam *after* the turning point that follows his passionate avowal to his mother and fight with his father: " '. . . You see I can give you a spirit love, I have given it you this long, long time; but not embodied passion. See, you are a nun. I have given you what I would give a holy nun—as a mystic monk to a holy nun.' "[25] Again this is a symbol based on actuality. E. T. records a letter Lawrence sent her: " 'Look, you are a nun. I give you what I would give a holy nun. You must let me marry a woman I can kiss and embrace and make the mother of my children.' "[26]

Having raised Miriam to the status of the virgin mother, Paul, because of his sexual repression, is full of "resentment at her repulses." Jones defines the same situation in *Hamlet*:

> His resentment against women is still further inflamed by the hypocritical prudishness with which Ophelia follows her father and brother in seeing evil in his natural affection, an attitude which poisons his love in exactly the same way that the love of his childhood, like that of all children must have been poisoned.[27]

Miriam follows her Father in heaven, her religiosity, and her mother, for whom sex is "always dreadful, but you have to bear it." But the result, Paul's Hamlet-like, disproportionate outbursts of rage against her, is the same. In the following most notable passage the naturalism of the act is fused with the phallic symbolism of the things described and the action itself. Miriam is slow to learn (ignorance is the intellectual abstract of virginity), and Paul, who is trying to teach her algebra, becomes impatient with her:

> She never reproached him or was angry with him. He was often cruelly ashamed. But still again his anger burst like a bubble surcharged; and still, when he saw her eager, silent, as it were, blind face, he felt he wanted to throw the pencil in it;

and still, when he saw her hand trembling and her mouth parted with suffering, his heart was scalded with pain for her. And because of the intensity to which she roused him, he sought her.[28]

The cause for this emotional schism is more apparent immediately following the clarifying scene between Paul and Gertrude and Walter Morel. The chapter "Defeat of Miriam" begins:

Paul was dissatisfied with himself and with everything. [Man delights me not, no, nor woman neither.] The deepest of his love belonged to his mother. When he felt he had hurt her, or wounded his love for her, he could not bear it. Now it was spring and there was battle between him and Miriam.[29]

The juxtaposition here of a consciously made choice of a loved object, Paul's mother, with whom only an attenuated spiritual communion would be possible, and a resolution to do "battle" with another loved object, with whom more than this communion would eventually be possible, suggests an identification of the two. In Paul's mind Miriam has become too firmly established as a mother surrogate. He must shake her loose. His final desperate suggestion to her that they become lovers represents the attempt to dislodge his mother from Miriam, the young girl, "full-breasted and luxuriantly formed." But even this wish, when it is granted, fails, and Paul remains, with her, Oedipus, doomed perpetually to stand on the steps of the palace and abide his incest.

From the very beginning Lawrence assigns to Miriam the maternal attributes that so embittered the real woman behind her. He makes her love Paul because he has been ill:

Then he was so ill, and she felt he would be weak. Then she would be stronger than he. Then she could love him. If she could be mistress of him in his weakness, take care of him, if he could depend on her, if she could, as it were. have him in her arms, how she could love him.[30]

She is referred to as the "threshing floor" of his ideas. Like Gertrude, who triumphs with him over his winning of a prize, Miriam is his means of conceiving. But all these births are virgin births; the real encounter, gross and physical, is beyond him. In terms of the conditions Freud sets up for the Oedipal type, Paul, torn between a repressed hostility and identification with his father, actually "rescues" Miriam from himself.

What points first to the "rescue" situation is Paul's peculiar rebelliousness toward his mother's values as his sexual drives increase in intensity. He becomes, for example, the champion of the common people, his father's class, because from them one gets "life itself, warmth, you feel their hates and loves." And Mrs. Morel retorts, "Why don't you go and talk to your father's pals?" It is from this man that Paul must save Miriam.

In a sociological excursus Lawrence describes Paul as a type:

> Being the sons of mothers whose husbands had blundered rather brutally through their feminine sanctities, they were themselves too diffident and shy. They could easier deny themselves than incur any reproach from a woman; for a woman was like their mother, and they were full of the sense of their mother.[31]

Paul's entire relationship with Miriam is the unconscious purgation of his own attitude toward her, accomplished by attributing to her that same attitude, which accurately describes his infantile need for love. Needing her love, yet unable to accept it, he accuses her of the same thing Gertrude Morel accused her of, of "sucking" the soul out of him:

> "You don't want to love—your eternal and abnormal craving is to be loved. You aren't positive, you're negative. You absorb, absorb, as if you must fill yourself up with love, because you've got a shortage somewhere." She was stunned by his cruelty.[32]

What is actually tormenting him in Miriam is the exact opposite of this accusation. It is that for the first time in his life he is facing a mature relationship between himself and another woman, *not* his mother, and that a different mode of love is being demanded from him. It is Miriam's refusal to allow him to regress to the Nirvana, the paradisal state of the infant, her insistence that he recognize her, that fills him with anguish. His further accusation of Miriam clarifies this. Paul makes his plea for the impersonality of passion, which Miriam denies him:

> Never any relaxing, never any leaving himself to the great hunger and impersonality of passion; he must be brought back to a deliberate, reflective creature. As if from a swoon of passion she called him back to the littleness of the personal relationship. He could not bear it. "Leave me alone—leave me alone!" he wanted to cry; but she wanted him to look at her with eyes full of love. His eyes full of the dark impersonal fire of desire, did not belong to her.
>
> "To be rid of our individuality, which is our will, which is our effort—to live effortless, a kind of conscious sleep—that is very beautiful, I think; that is our afterlife—our immortality."[33]

Here in these few sentences is an adumbration of that "drift toward death" as Lawrence sublimated it into the passional relationship par excellence between men and women. But implicit in it here is the ultimate regression to the child's status with its mother. In his final achievement of a sexual union between them, Paul, more strongly than ever, identifies Miriam with his mother—but not his mother alive, in spite of the fact that her death is still remote; that identification would be too painful. Just as his mother's lips were cold to his passionate kiss, he realizes, after his orgasm, that Miriam "had not been with him all the time, that her soul had stood apart in a sort of horror." But still with this virginal woman there is a pleasure:

He, as he lay on his face on the dead pine leaves, felt ex-
traordinarily quiet. He did not mind if the raindrops came on
him: he would have lain and got wet through: he felt as if
nothing mattered, as if his living were smeared away into the
beyond, near and quite lovable. This strange reaching out to
death was new to him. . . .

   To him now, life seemed a shadow, day a white shadow;
night, and day, and stillness and inaction, this seemed like
being. To be alive, to be urgent and insistent—that was *not-
to-be*. The highest of all was to melt out into the darkness
and sway there, identified with the great Being.[34]

The pleasure is deadly: the road to Thebes again, which
for a moment he agrees to take, and which, in the end, he
will not take. In the end the same wish is distasteful to him,
and described in a tone of horror, after his mother's death:
". . . the tear in the veil, through which his life seemed to
drift slowly, as if he were drawn toward death. He wanted
someone of their own free initiative to help him."[35] But
in his first intercourse with Miriam he seems to be insisting
that she be a mother before she has a name. The artist
seems unconsciously to be trying, with his mother's death,
to find some sexual substitute for it, describing in Miriam's
frigidity the more tolerable mask of a repressed necrophilia,
a desire to be at any cost with his mother. Because these things
are latent in his relationship with Miriam, it is imperative
that Paul cast her off. As with his own mother, Paul cannot
get "at her" either in life or death.

   The curiously withering, deathlike nature of Paul's pleasure after Miriam's defloration will continue to echo through
Lawrence's works. Freud offers an interesting insight into
the reactions of an artist whose young manhood was spent
in an atmosphere of such virginal purity. Freud speaks of
the primitive taboos of virginity as deriving from the
ambivalent nature of the act of defloration—the inflicting
of pain instead of pleasure upon the woman one marries—

and so incurring in a love object emotions of hostility and the desire to return evil for evil by destroying the man:

> Perhaps this dread is based on the fact that woman is different from man, for ever incomprehensible and mysterious, strange, and therefore apparently hostile. The man is afraid of being weakened by the woman, infected with her femininity, and of then showing himself incapable. The effect which coitus has of discharging tensions and causing flaccidity may be the prototype of what the man fears; and realization of the influence which the woman gains over him through sexual intercourse, the consideration she thereby forces from him, may justify the extension of the fear. In all this there is nothing obsolete, nothing which is not still alive among ourselves.[36]

With his growing tendency in his sexual relations to equate himself with his father, Paul has in the example of his mother not only the woman who took his father's strength from him and made him "paltry and insignificant," but the additional threat of the cold, puritanical woman, the virgin, who does not experience the "flaccidity" of the father, and who emerges from their "acts of violence" the moral victor. Of both these virginal qualities Miriam is the obvious continuation. Her purity triumphs hatefully over his weakness, nor will she permit him the escape advantage of regression into "impersonality."

Paul misses in Miriam-as-mother the presence of the "injured third party" and tries, as he tried to shift his own emotional passivity, to thrust Miriam into the maternal situation. His attempts follow, as we can almost predict they will follow, the "recognition" scene with his parents. The offering of the role is disguised as a tender concern, the wish that Miriam would become interested in someone else, for fear her family would insist upon a formal engagement. "Do you think—if I didn't come up so much—you might get to like somebody else—another man?" The attempts fail, and with the failure the relationship, in Freudian terms, loses one of its most important underpinnings.

While Miriam cannot produce an "injured third party" to satisfy Paul's unconscious need for a rival, she is capable of fulfilling the mother-love role in another way, which is an even more striking insight into the true nature of Paul's relationships with all three women. Throughout *Sons and Lovers* we notice a chiasmus of "giving," on the parts of the women, with varying shades of approval and disapproval. The first woman to give is of course Gertrude. She "gives" William's girls to Walter Morel by purposely confusing the father and son. In the repressed phantasy of the son the act appears to be a diverting of the father that leaves the mother free for the son. Later, with great reluctance she gives William up to the girl he is engaged to. But the results are fatal.

Miriam's act of giving coincides exactly with Gertrude Morel's approval of Clara for Paul, as something he needs, as something neither of them can give him. Gertrude, considering Clara, refuses to define her approval: "She did not know what she wished, but left it vague. At any rate she was not hostile to the idea of Clara." Miriam's recognition disguises itself as a struggle between higher and lower natures:

> So in May she asked him to come to Willey Farm and meet Mrs. Dawes. There was something he hankered after. She saw him, whenever they spoke of Clara Dawes, rouse and get slightly angry. He said he did not like her. Yet he was keen to know about her. Well, he should put himself to the test. She believed that there were in him desires for higher things, and desires for lower, and that the desires for the higher would conquer. At any rate, he should try.[37]

It is a recapitulation of Gertrude Morel's reluctant giving of William to Lily, which constitutes in effect the necessary condition for such a union—the acceptance from the mother's hand of her successor.

When Paul and Clara and Miriam are together, Miriam falls into the role of the Gertrude who disapproves of dancing and of sexual desires. And Paul, treating Miriam exactly as if she were his mother, pantomimically makes his escape: "He was utterly unfaithful to her even in her own presence; then he was ashamed, then repentant; then he hated her, and went off again. Those were the ever-recurring conditions."[38]

But Clara, too, is a surrogate mother, the opposite of Gertrude and Miriam, the "harlot," the possession of another. It is from her hands that Paul receives, not the virginal Miriam, but the sexually obtainable Miriam. Before she sleeps with Paul, Clara symbolically introduces Paul to sex. She tells him, in effect, what the real relations between his parents are. Paul insists that Miriam wants only a "soul union."

> "How do you know what she is?"
> "I do! I know she wants a sort of soul union."
> "But how do you know what she wants?"
> "I've been with her for seven years."
> "And you haven't found out the first thing about her."
> "What's that?"
> "That she doesn't want any of your soul communion. That's your imagination. She wants you."
> He pondered over this. Perhaps he was wrong.
> "But she seems—" he began.
> "You've never tried," she answered.[39]

"With the spring came again the old madness and battle," starts the next chapter, called "The Test on Miriam." It is full of the imagery of the impenetrable hymen, against which Paul, armed with knowledge, must force himself. There is an "obstacle," "physical bondage," virginity as a "positive force," so "hard to overcome," something Paul must "deliberately break through." Paul fears the "sacrifice" of himself in marriage as "degrading." In giving Paul to Miriam, before taking him herself, Clara is like Queen Gertrude, and Paul like Hamlet. Clara's sexual knowledge-ableness inspires Paul to talk to the "nunlike" Miriam of "country matters" for the first time, suggesting that they become lovers. " 'Sometime you will have me?' he murmured [note the passivity of the speaker], hiding his face on her shoulder. It was so difficult."[40] And when the affair is disastrous, and the "dead" Miriam gives Paul back to Clara, Clara strews Miriam's grave with contempt. She agrees with Gertrude Morel about her. "What I hate is the bloodhound quality in Miriam," she tells Paul's mother, and Paul, angry, yet in agreement with her, buries Miriam forever.

The shift from Miriam to Clara is the shift from *mater urania* to *mater pandemos*.[41] Miriam is the incomplete metamorphosis of the real mother to her unconsciously idealized form. Miriam resembles Gertrude in purity and intellectuality and protectiveness. With Clara the metamorphosis is complete; we can no longer refer her maternal qualities to some real person, but must look to some elemental concept of maternity and orgiastic sexuality as one sees it in the chthonic goddesses, Cybele, Ishtar, Hertha. The transition from Miriam to Clara is rendered florally. Paul walks in the garden. The madonna lilies, the flowers that consoled his mother, call to him with their scents, but he ignores them:

> Behind him the great flowers leaned as if they were calling. And then, like a shock, he caught another perfume, something raw and coarse. Hunting round, he found the purple iris, touched their fleshy throats and their dark, grasping hands. At any rate, he had found something. They stood stiff in the darkness. Their scent was brutal. The moon was melting down upon the crest of the hill. It was gone; all was dark. The corn-crake called still.[42]

❊

Paul's relationship with Miriam fails because his repressed image of the beloved is fundamentally denied him. Like Ophelia she is sexually desirable, or should be, but her virginity is a supreme article of her desirability. With her as with his mother, Paul cannot act out the desired incest. His relationship with Clara, on the other hand, succeeds and fails in turn because his repressed image of the beloved mother is realized in every essential. With Miriam, who was an actual person, the life situation as it might have been appeals to conscious experience. Clara, whom E. T. describes as a "clever adaptation of elements from three people. The events related had no foundation in fact,"[43] speaks to the artist's unconscious wishes. Hence the almost rigidly determined nature of Paul's relationship with her.

Clara fulfills all the conditions Freud describes as proper to her being chosen by Paul. She is the possession of another man, the "injured third party," Baxter Dawes, from whom it seems desirable that Paul "rescue" her. Paul suddenly realizes her vulnerability when they first meet, her need to be rescued: "Suddenly looking at her, he saw that the upward lifting of her face was misery and not scorn. His heart grew tender for everybody. He turned and was gentle with Miriam whom he had neglected till then."[44] In the perfect grasp he has of this sudden reaction there is implicit the further desire by Paul that Clara be a fallen woman, Magdalen, the "harlot." Before this he has recognized her sensual appeal to him. " 'Look at her mouth—made for passion and the very setback of her throat'—He threw his head back in Clara's definite manner."[45]

When Paul visits Clara and sees the shabbiness of her life he is unconsciously excited by the notion of "rescue":

He experienced a thrill of joy, thinking she might need his help. She seemed denied and deprived of so much. And her arm moved mechanically, that should never have been subdued to a mechanism, and her head was bowed to the lace that never should have been bowed. She seemed to be stranded there among the refuse that life has thrown away, doing her jennying. . . . Her grey eyes at last met his. They looked dumb with humiliation, pleading with a kind of captive misery. He was shaken and at a loss. He had thought her high and mighty.[46]

Seated at her lacework she seems to Paul a Penelope, waiting. The image is apt, for it is again the waiting mother in need of a rescue, to which Telemachus dedicates himself. Paul sees her also as a "Juno dethroned," a comparison that introduces another remarkable series of descriptive terms applied to Clara. One infallible sign of a divinity, either male or female, according to Greek religious belief, was the slightly larger than human size of the visitant. According to Freudian theory the giants of the world's mythologies originated in the infantile phantasies concerning adults, parents especially, the memories of a time when certain human beings were regularly huge and terrifyingly capable of lifting one up bodily. Shakespeare's Venus—

> Over one arm the lusty courser's rein,
> Under the other was the tender boy—

is the love-enthralled Titan with Adonis. To Clara, Lawrence applies the images of giantism. Paul sees under her clothes "her strong form that seemed to slumber with power."[47] He sees her hand, "large, to match her large limbs," in contrast to his own smaller, delicate hands. He feels her heavy shoulder upon him, her "white, heavy arms." "There was no himself. The grey and black eyes of Clara, her bosom coming down on him. . . . Then he felt himself small and helpless, her towering in her force above him."[48] So in this "composite" imaginary woman Lawrence gathers the attributes of the Great Mother par excellence, "her bosom coming down on him"; what Freud calls "the memory picture of his mother as it has dominated him since the beginning of childhood."

In their sexual intercourse Lawrence carries on the ideal-izing process, "the way of phantasies." It is a kind of inter-course the real Miriam would not allow him to have, the paradisal situation (Paradise is mentioned) in which there is no consciousness:

> To know their own nothingness, to know the tremendous living flood which carried them always, gave them rest within themselves. If so great a magnificent power could overwhelm them, identify them altogether with itself, so that they knew they were only grains in the tremendous heave that lifted every grass blade its little height, and every tree, and living thing, then why fret about themselves? They could let themselves be carried by life. . . .[49]

But underneath the stock vitalism there lurks the same passive yielding that characterized his intercourse with Miriam. The difference lies in the role Clara plays as the "harlot" of phantasy. Freud expands the harlot theme in another essay to explain the phenomenon of psychical im-potence in terms of the "incest-barrier" and steps taken to overcome it. One step is to separate the lust object from the love object, i.e., the harlot from the madonna:

> The whole sphere of love in such people remains divided in the two directions personified in art as sacred and profane (or animal) love. Where they love they do not desire and where they desire they cannot love. They seek objects which they do not need to love, in order to keep their sensuality away from the objects they love; and, in accordance with the laws of the "complexive sensitiveness" and of the return of the repressed, the strange failure shown in psychical impotence makes its appearance whenever an object which has been chosen with the aim of avoiding incest recalls the prohibited object through some feature, often an inconspicuous one.
>
> The main protective measure against such a disturbance which men have recourse to in this split in their love consists in a physical *debasement* of the sexual object, the overvalua-tion that normally attaches to the sexual object being reserved for the incestuous object and its representatives. As soon as

the condition of debasement is fulfilled, sensuality can be freely expressed, and important sexual capacities and a high degree of sexual pleasure can develop. There is a further factor which contributes to this result. People in whom there has not been a proper confluence of the affectionate and the sensual currents do not usually show much refinement in their modes of behaviour in love; they have retained perverse sexual aims whose nonfulfillment is felt as a serious loss of pleasure, and whose fulfillment on the other hand seems possible only with a debased and despised sexual object.

We can now understand the motives behind the . . . phantasies . . . which degrade the mother to the level of a prostitute. They are efforts to bridge the gulf between the two currents in love, at any rate in phantasy, and by debasing the mother to acquire her as an object of sensuality. . . . I do not hesitate to make the two factors at work in psychical impotence in the strict sense—the factors of intense incestuous fixation in childhood and the frustration by reality in adolescence—responsible too, for this extremely common characteristic of the love of civilized men.[50]

In terms of the above-quoted passage Paul's affair with Clara falls within a predictable pattern of behavior, compatible with the other actions of the protagonist. Relieved for the moment, with this beautiful "composite," of the incestuous identification, Paul lapses into the very pleasurable but extremely regressive pleasure of the "nothingness" passion can reduce him to, closely related to the "reaching out to death" of his affair with Miriam. Then, because Clara is, even more than Miriam, the product of an incestuous synthesis, the "return of the repressed" reasserts itself:

Their loving grew more mechanical, without the marvellous glamour. Gradually they began to introduce novelties to get back some of the feeling of satisfaction. . . . And afterward each of them was rather ashamed, and these things caused a distance between the two of them. He began to despise her a little, as if she had merited it![51]

Part of the "debasement" of the object involves, I believe, an element of self-debasement or, if debasement is not the exact term, an attempt to achieve a callousness of sensibility which will make the woman's debasement acceptable. In this case, the refined, sensitive Paul, in the very beginning, which is the most exciting phase of his affair with Clara, lapses into his father's Midland dialect after he has been with Clara on the raw, red, clay bank of the Trent in flood, as if this gross, sexual act had been the *rite de passage* that put him on terms of equality with his father. The brutal natural surroundings, so unlike the soft meadow and pine forest of Miriam's defloration, and the scattered red petals of the carnation, a dream symbol of the menses, speak for the degradation both of the woman into adultery and of the man into the coarser, less sensitive state of manhood. But afterward, as if to reassert his status as the son, Paul, just as he did with Gertrude, insists upon cleaning Clara's boots. The harlot-mother identification is completed. "'And now I'll clean thy boots and make thee fit for respectable folk,' he said."[52] Paul had cleaned his mother's boots "with as much reverence as if they had been flowers." Not that his mother's shoes needed cleaning. "Mrs. Morel was one of those naturally exquisite people who can walk in mud without dirtying their shoes."[53] In the light of this comparison the boot cleaning becomes a ritual, like the raising of Magdalen to the level of Mary. Gertrude's sexual "shoes" (compare the removal of shoes as a sign of refusal to marry in the Bible in Deuteronomy 25:6) are not dirty, even though she has borne children. Clara's shoes, after her intercourse with Paul, must be cleaned. The act raises her to the status of mother as well as mistress. Freud points out the fetishism connected with the foot as a very primitive sexual symbol and notes the aptness of the shoe as a symbol for the female genitals.

Similarly, Lawrence places a peculiar emphasis on the taking off of collars. In *Sons and Lovers* the phallic significance of the collar is connected with Gertrude Morel's hold upon her husband and her children. Walter Morel's shame before her, after he has fought with her and locked her out, is an acknowledgment of her moral superiority and her mastery of him. When she enters the house he takes flight: ". . . she saw him almost running through the door to the stairs. He had ripped his collar off his neck in his haste to be gone ere she came in, and there it lay with bursten button holes. It made her angry."[54]

William, her first favorite, loves his collar:

> She liked to do things for him; she liked to put a cup for his tea and to iron his collar, of which he was so proud. It was a joy to her to have him proud of his collars. There was no laundry. So she used to rub away at them with her little convex iron, to polish them till they shone from the sheer pressure of her arm.[55]

The collar figures in his death:

> On the Sunday morning as he was putting his collar on:
> "Look," he said to his mother, holding up his chin, "What a rash my collar's made under my chin!"
> Just at the junction of chin and throat was a big red inflammation.[56]

It is the lesion of the disease that kills him.

In the scene between Paul and his mother that ends in his fight with his father, Gertrude openly expresses her jealousy of Miriam, and Paul insists to her that he does not love her:

> "No, mother—I really *don't* love her. I talk to her, but I want to come home to you."
> He had taken off his collar and tie, and rose, bare-throated, to go to bed. As he stooped to kiss his mother, she threw her arms round his neck, hid her face on his shoulder, and cried in a whimpering voice, so unlike her own that he writhed in agony.[57]

Now the collar has become Gertrude. (In *Aaron's Rod*, Aaron tears himself away from the sexual bondage of his wife

Lotte. In one struggle between them he escapes, leaving his torn collar behind in her hand.[58])

With the dying of Paul's mother, Paul's sexuality begins to equate itself more and more with actual death. Like Dostoevsky's epileptic seizures, whose psychogenic origin Freud founds in a pantomime of his father's death, Paul's orgasm in Clara's arms is a little death.

> When he had her then, there was something in it that made her shrink away from him—something unnatural. She grew to dread him. He was so quiet, yet so strange. She was afraid of the man who was not there with her, whom she could feel behind this make-belief lover; somebody sinister, that filled her with horror. She began to have a kind of horror of him. It was almost as if he were a criminal. He wanted her—he had her—and it made her feel as if death itself had her in its grip. She lay in horror.[59]

With Paul's last embrace of a living woman all three women are finally joined and identified as one, the mother. When she dies, the regressive, incestuous phantasies her life had fed sicken and die with her. The pleasantly deathly consummation with Miriam and the Nirvana-like "impersonality of passion" with Clara resolve themselves in Paul's horror at the coldness of his mother's lips, a horror he inverts and feels in Clara when he lies with her. Gertrude's death releases both Clara and Miriam from their functions as mother surrogates. They do not die for Paul; it is he, finally, who samples death, first pantomiming it in Clara's arms and, at the last, feeling it on his mother's mouth. Clara's horror of him is based on this: that Paul is trying to "die" on her.

In the end Paul rejects death; *Sons and Lovers* is a comedy of the Oedipus complex. He is not Oedipus standing on the steps of his stricken house—he is journeying forth. Even the blindness is touched upon. Paul is described as turning "blindly." "He dared not meet his own eyes in the mirror. He never looked at himself."[60] But the rejection of death is positive and absolute, and in its rejection, perverse as it may seem, is the implicit rejection, valid in unconscious terms, of the women to whom he might have turned after the long night of his childhood was past. By rejecting Miriam and Clara, Paul dramatically represents to himself the profound change that has come over him. Fiction is invoked to dispel what in real life might have been an attenuating relationship, and to put in its place a more dramatic *hic incipit vita nova.*

When Miriam, out of compassion, asks him to marry her, his reply shows the extent of his knowledge of what has happened. "But—you love me so much, you want to put me in your pocket. And I should die there, smother."[61] The unconscious formulation of the reply is rather an expression on Paul's part of his refusal to be tempted to crawl into another pocket, now that the one he has been in for so long has worn out and left him free.

It is Paul's walk, on the last page of *Sons and Lovers,* toward the "faintly humming, glowing town" that sounds the note of positive choice. And the choice is, in psycho-analytic terms, a classically important one. In choosing the town Paul is accepting his father, an idealized image, like Hamlet's father, a "man," with all the expansive attributes the generic term allows. Turning his back upon his home place he is rejecting, or at least modifying, his acceptance of the mother. I think the process can be described as an inversion, a turning over to find a new center of gravity, long withheld. Whereas before Paul had, in the mother, loved an idealized image, capable of dangerous extensions into mother surrogates like Miriam and Clara, he had, in the father, hated (with that curious ambivalence, already noted) an identity, with a local habitation and a name. With Baxter Dawes, the process begins to reverse itself. The father's identity begins to be idealized and lose its historical boundaries in Walter Morel, while Gertrude

Morel is forced, by the exigencies of Paul's insistence upon becoming a man, into mere motherhood; and with this her surrogates lose their vitality and fall away.

From the very beginning the town stands in polar hostility to Gertrude, as the world of men, of deflowered countryside. It is to the town that Walter Morel and Jerry Purdy take their pub-crawling walk. The "wakes" is a part of town life, the first sounds, for young William Morel, of the outside world: "the braying of a merry-go-round and the tooting of a horn." Gertrude hates the wakes, and Lawrence describes William, crucified by a choice, who "stood watching her, cut to the heart to let her go, and yet unable to leave the wakes." For Paul in his turn the town exercises its attraction: "From the train going home at night he used to watch the lights of the town, sprinkled thick on the hills, fusing together in a blaze in the valleys. He felt rich in life and happy."[62] Like the "stars and sun, a few bright grains . . . holding each other in embrace," the town defies the dark, sometimes horrible, onetime appeal of the maternal invitation to be still and passive. It is, like all the towers, citadels, mountaintops, and Beautiful Cities of literature, the place to which one fights his way through the seas and jungles of world or mind.

In the end of *Sons and Lovers* is implicit an acceptance of the father's values. Oedipus says, in what is the essential irony of the play: "In doing right by Laius I protected myself, for whoever slew Laius might turn a hand against me." Paul Morel is categorically rejecting all the elements of his Oedipal involvement. Having restored the Player King, Baxter Dawes, to his Player Queen, Clara, he enters the town, a man both driven and drawn across the threshold into manhood. In ratifying finally the bents and needs of the father, he "protects" himself.

·IV

THE

GREAT

CIRCLE

IN 1913 the young D. H. Lawrence wrote a story about Prussian militarism. Its first title was "Honour and Arms"; we know it as "The Prussian Officer." It was received with the praise it deserved as a profound criticism of a form of brutality for which Prussianism became a synonym. There seems to be nothing extraordinary about its genesis; it was the product of sensitive, first-hand observation.

Lawrence was traveling in Bavaria with the woman who was later to become his wife, Frieda von Richtofen Weekley. There his experiences with Prussianism were numerous and varied. Frieda's father, the old Baron von Richtofen, was a retired officer, a man who assumed that Prussian discipline was the *sine qua non* of manliness. Frieda herself had told him of what she had seen of Prussian army life. In addition, several notorious instances of brutality had aroused indignation throughout the Reich, such as the "Zabern Affair," in which an officer had sabered a lame cobbler, and rumors about the overt and suppressed homosexuality in the Prussian army were prevalent at the time.

It was such cases as these that Sandor Ferenczi alludes to in his essay on homoerotism of 1914, when he writes:

69

> In primitive peoples and among even the highly civilized
> Greeks amphi-erotism was an acceptable form of gratification.
> . . . In Europe men have lost the capacity for mutual affection
> and amiability. . . . I would even go so far as to regard the
> barbarous duels of the German students as similarly distorted
> proofs of affection towards members of their own sex.[1]

Nor does it seem too astonishing that Lawrence should have
grasped this insight into the nature of Prussianism; it is
one he appears to have worked out at least once before
in connection with a play, *Jeanne d'Arc*, by his friend and
publisher, Edward Garnett. To Garnett he wrote, apropos
of the play:

> Cruelty is a form of perverted sex. I want to dogmatize.
> Priests in their celibacy get their sex lustful, then perverted,
> then insane, hence Inquisitions—all sexual in origin. And
> soldiers, being herded together, men without women, never
> being *satisfied*, as a man never is from a street affair, get their
> surplus sex and their frustration and dissatisfaction into the
> blood, and *love* cruelty. It is sex lust fermented makes atrocity.[2]

This is hardly a Freudian explanation, but it is a valid one,
nonetheless. It was not likely that Lawrence, who wrote
Katherine Mansfield once, "Ask Freud or Jung about it?
Never!" would have dulled the bright immediacy of one of
his intuitions with the laboriously responsible methods of
Freudian analysis.

The "Prussian Officer" describes an obscene struggle between two men. The one, an officer, his homoerotic impulses
inflamed by his military right to the absolute domination of
his young orderly, and by the orderly's own complete submission to him, treats the orderly cruelly, kicking and abus-
ing him and at the same time exhibiting the most morbid
curiosity as to the orderly's own life. The orderly's scarred
thumb is an object of interest to the officer. "He wanted to
get hold of it and—a hot flame ran in his blood." The
orderly's poem to his girl arouses his anger, and the officer
forbids him to see her again. "The officer tried hard not to

admit the passion that had got hold of him. He would not know that his feeling for his orderly was anything but that of a man incensed by his stupid, perverse servant."[3]

Lawrence's physical description of the officer is perfunctory, but telling:

> He was a Prussian aristocrat, haughty and overbearing. But his mother had been a Polish countess. Having made too many gambling debts when he was young, he had ruined his prospects in the Army and remained an infantry captain. He had never married. . . . Now and then he took himself a mistress. But after such an event he returned to his duty still more hostile and irritable.[4]

The orderly is in direct contrast to the officer:

> . . . a youth of about twenty-two, of medium height, and well built. He had strong, heavy limbs, was swarthy, with a soft, black, young moustache. There was something altogether warm and young about him. He had firmly marked eyebrows over dark, expressionless eyes, that seemed never to have thought, only to have received life direct through his senses and acted straight from instinct.[5]

But Lawrence is not satisfied to deal in the flat characterizations of aristocratic sadist and proletarian victim. The psychological complexities appear as nuances, but are there nevertheless, the tacit response of the orderly to the unspeakable relationship the captain offers him. The orderly's submission has in it the feminine qualities of self-surrender and passive acceptance, even admiration: "His orderly having to rub him down, admired the amazing riding-muscles of his loins."[6] We are being conditioned throughout the story to accept the actions of both men in their relations with each other as ambivalent. The obsession of the officer with the orderly's thumb and with kicking him always in the thighs and buttocks finds its corollary in the orderly's passivity in the face of punishment and his admiration for the officer's riding muscles. Both men experience physical excitement in each other's presence. "The officer's heart was plunging." "The officer could hear him [the orderly] panting."

The end of the story is the consummation of this relationship, a real love-death. The orderly as well as the officer accepts the bloody substitute for love the officer holds out. He has feared "a personal interchange with his master," but finally it comes. He shares the terrible intercourse, which shows itself in both as cruelty and murder.

The orderly is wakened to action by the sight of the officer drinking, his throat, "moving up and down as he drank, the strong jaw working."

> And in a second the orderly with serious earnest young face, and underlip between his teeth, had got his knee in the officer's chest and was pressing the chin backward over the farther edge of the tree-stump, pressing, with all his heart behind in a passion of relief, the tension of his wrists exquisite with relief. And with the base of his palms he shoved at the chin, with all his might. And it was pleasant, too, to have that chin, that hard jaw, already slightly rough with beard, in his hands. . . . Heavy convulsions shook the body of the officer, frightening and horrifying the young soldier. Yet it pleased him, too, to repress them. It pleased him to keep his hands pressing back the chin, to feel the chest of the other man yield in expiration to the weight of his strong young knees, to feel the hard twitchings of the prostrate body jerking his own whole frame, which was pressed down on it.[7]

After he has killed the officer he feels, not remorse, but a morbid solicitude for him: "He could not bear to see the long, military body lying broken over the tree-base . . . he pushed the limbs straight and decent."[8] And his last thoughts turn to the man he killed: "then the pang of hate for the Captain, followed by a pang of tenderness and ease."[9]

Considered in isolation "The Prussian Officer" is a masterpiece of observed reality, both external, in connection with the cultural basis for its action, and internal, with regard to the history and the personality of the officer. Rarely does tragic inevitability identify itself so closely and with such clarity with psychological inevitability in a work of art.

It is specifically in connection with the psychological quality of the action that we begin to question the extent to which "observed reality" was responsible for the final excellence of this story. Lawrence rarely deals in his fiction with exotic heroes; an Italian, an Indian, a German almost make up the lot. Removed as it is from Lawrence's life, "The Prussian Officer," with its effortless handling of the perverse relationship between the two men, urges upon us the conclusion that conscious art, even intuition, is less important here than the frank exercise of what might be called psychoanalytic confession. It is the artist's valuable prerogative to extend his experience through the explorations of what in the merely neurotic would amount to symptoms and reaction formations.

It is when we collate the events and characters in "The Prussian Officer" with the events and characters in some of Lawrence's other works that the fact emerges that Lawrence is working always with analogues drawn from his own life.

> I write every book three times [Lawrence told a friend]. By that I don't mean copying and revising as I go along, but literally. After I finish the first draft I put it aside and write another. Then I put the second aside and write a third. The first draft is generally somewhat like *Sons and Lovers*.[10]

I have said earlier that Lawrence in *Sons and Lovers*, while attempting to make what appears to be a conscious analysis of his Oedipal relationships, achieved on an unconscious level ends that far outstripped his conscious intention. For Lawrence the accomplishment of *Sons and Lovers*, his first and most direct exploration of the Oedipal relationship, constitutes not so much the exhaustion of that exploration as it does a psychological meridian of Greenwich from which all other explorations must be conducted and to which they must return in that great circle course Lawrence's mind pursued. Freud's beautiful phrase, "the return of the repressed," aptly describes the thematic continuity of Lawrence's work.

I proposed in my study of *Sons and Lovers* that Paul Morel's loves and rivalries are categorically determined by the original family situation from which he cannot extricate himself.[11] The two women in Paul's life, the virginal Miriam and the Junoesque Clara Dawes, divide the mother's identity between them. Miriam, because she comes closer to approximating the moral and intellectual superiority of his mother, constitutes the sexually inaccessible half of this complete mother. She is the "virtuous and respectable woman" Freud describes.[12]

Clara Dawes constitutes, on the other hand, the "sexually discredited" woman who must be "rescued" from a lover or husband, anyone who can claim some right to possess her. She also satisfies other unconscious requirements made of her. She is intellectually superior to her husband, whom she has rejected. In her role as the fallen woman she is sexually accessible; it is with her that the young man first can realize erotic passion. And it is her husband, Baxter Dawes, who constitutes the extension into Paul's adult life of the despised father. Both are laborers; both are pungently and, for Paul, offensively and yet attractively male, as he himself is not.

In connection with "The Prussian Officer" it is these two men who command our interest. They are, to begin with, physical and social prototypes of the orderly. They are from the lower classes. In *Sons and Lovers* Paul does not accept them with the magnanimity with which Lawrence will accept the orderly; they are his brutal father and his inferior rival. But he has an abstract approval of them: "Only from the middle class one gets ideas, and from the common people—life itself, warmth. You feel their hates and loves."[13] In his description of Paul Morel's father Lawrence invokes the same picture of unconscious instinctive vitality that he will use in his portrayal of the orderly.[14] The other man, Baxter Dawes, has the same quality that Paul Morel's father has, the mindlessness on which Lawrence was to place such value in his works. His good looks, strength, his "white skin with a clear, golden tinge," his dark eyes, and his primitive directness place him in the father's category.

Toward Dawes, Paul Morel exhibits the same ambivalences of love and hate, hostility and morbid solicitude he had previously shown for his father. In both cases the son's attitude is revealing of the repressed hostility latent in Paul Morel's attitude toward the biological and the surrogate father. "Paul had a curious sensation of pity almost of affection mingled with violent hate for the man."[15] The relationship between the two men culminates in a conflict identical, except in two significant respects, to the conflict that terminates "The Prussian Officer." Dawes, the rejected husband, waylays Paul Morel in the fields and attacks him physically. The young man, in desperation, gets the upper hand.[16] Paul gives up his hold on Dawes and allows himself to be kicked into unconsciousness. His only thought after this is to return to his mother. He gives up Clara as his mistress and returns her to her husband.

The difference between this struggle and the orderly's killing of the officer rests essentially on the unconscious realignment of the characters in "The Prussian Officer."

Sons and Lovers is where we begin. The less fully resolved relationship between the father and son in that novel is the relationship upon whose psychic residue Lawrence was to draw for the rest of his life. Indeed, his first task after *Sons and Lovers* seems to have been the conciliation, with honor, of the father, a conciliation that proceeds in a steady line of descent from father to rival, to friend, to positive identity between the father image and the son. Our understanding of the process makes for an insight into the characterology of Lawrence's protagonists, who tend steadily and progressively toward a fusion of these filial and paternal strains. Setting before us the action of "The Prussian Officer" as the literary resolution of the problem, I should like to develop systematically the steps Lawrence took toward the making of that story.

In *Sons and Lovers* we are aware only of the conflict, a recurrent pattern, a sadomasochistic phantasy in which the unequivocal son is beaten by the unequivocal father for daring to possess the mother. The son then retaliates by strangling the father. In *Sons and Lovers* Paul Morel makes the parricidal gesture against his rival, Baxter Dawes; denies it; allows himself to be beaten; and, in full flight, gives up his rivalry and regresses to his old dependency on his mother, once more a child.

This partial parricide and final submission reveal another aspect of the phantasy. In the aggressive or sexual source of the son's hostility toward the father lies the son's tendency to *become* the brutal father. Immediately the scruple of love for and fear of the father causes a suppression of this brutal image and the subsequent turning upon oneself. The sadistic component involves identification with the father; the masochistic component, the inverted Oedipus pattern, involves a submission to the good father image and castration. In *Sons and Lovers* Paul Morel does not identify himself with his father; he renounces (we will save repression for Lawrence) his hostility and rivalry, and tacitly "ratifies" his father's gross, physical manhood.

In this sense *Sons and Lovers* is a pyrrhic victory; Paul Morel is derelict in the end, bereft of mother, mistress, father, and friend. With the disappearance of his field of action Paul Morel is no longer free to exercise his filial status. Lawrence had lost the short-lived protagonist who had carried him through *The White Peacock*, as Cyril, and through *Sons and Lovers*, as Paul Morel. In both these novels the father came off badly, but in both with a little catch of saving grace. In *The White Peacock* Cyril's father is the biological prototype for Walter Morel, except that in this novel it is not given him even to appear.

> The marriage had been unhappy. My father was of a frivolous, rather vulgar character, but plausible, having a great deal of charm. He was a liar, without notion of honesty, and he had deceived my mother thoroughly. One after another she discovered his mean dishonesties and deceits, and her soul revolted from him, and because the illusions of him had broken into a thousand vulgar fragments, she turned away with the scorn of a woman who finds her romance had been a trumpery tale.[17]

Although neither of these men seems to have much survival value as possible protagonists, it is with them in some idealized state that Lawrence will compound. The end of *Sons and Lovers*, then, marks the beginning of a search for "a friend or a lover" and, more than that, the finding among the ruins of the past of a more adequate selfhood than Paul Morel was able to provide. It is in this connection that Lawrence, in *The Prussian Officer*, the collection of short stories that followed *Sons and Lovers*, recapitulates, reconsiders, and reorders the events, characters, and moral judgments of *Sons and Lovers*.

The primary recapitulation of that novel consists of an almost systematic reassessment of the principals involved in it, setting the stage, clumsily, in many instances, for the artistic readjustments that must follow the new knowledge. *Sons and Lovers* has sounded depths; the next step must be to illuminate them, even to the point of being inartistically explicit. The achievement of his most important task—that conciliation, with honor, of the father—is beset with difficulties, involving the fine balance of antipathy with identification and love with fear and hatred. The conclusion, therefore, of such an early story as "The Christening" is a pastiche of conflicting attitudes. It shows the artist in the caldron of ambivalence, trying to isolate the pure essence of an emotion, trying not to faint back into the old parricidal ways of *Sons and Lovers*. Tenderness wars with resentment; the old man's confession is self-condemnatory, yet he is nobler in defeat than his children and more spiritually elect than the minister.

The old collier, broken with disease, is present at the christening of his daughter's illegitimate child. The minister has come to baptize it, but the ceremony is a travesty. The collier's son, "black in his pit dirt, grinning through the panes," mocks the service. The children are drawn apart in shame and bitterness. Suddenly the old man prays:

> For I have stood between Thee and my children; I've had *my* way with them, Lord; I've stood between Thee and my children; I've cut them off from Thee because they were mine. And they've grown twisted because of me. . . . Let me own it, Lord, I've done 'em mischief. It would ha' been better if they'd never known no father. . . . For I've been like a stone upon them, and they rise up and curse me in their wickedness.[18]

This naïve confession of guilt is lost on the children, who ascribe it to the old man's enfeeblement. It is also lost on the story; for all its vitality derives from the wider, less self-conscious stage of *Sons and Lovers*, and, perhaps, to judge by the last lines with their vivid image followed by a gesture of rejection, from one of Blake's visions of a father-twisted world.

> The day after the christening he staggered in at the doorway declaring in a loud voice with joy in life still: "The daisies light up the earth, they clap their hands in multitudes, in praise of the morning."
> And his daughters shrank, sullen.[19]

"The Christening" marks the beginning of some tentative identification with, if not the father himself, the father's position. It is an *entente cordiale,* a position to which the artist's unconscious tended throughout *Sons and Lovers,* but whose accomplishment was prevented by the more successful artifice of the father surrogate.

But the father of "The Christening" is an aging Walter Morel with a difference. He is articulate in his lyrical outburst, precise in the statement of his guilt. The note is not false; it is symptomatic of the process Lawrence's protagonists were to undergo. Literacy in his uncultured heroes is not merely a *deus ex machina* by which experience achieves conscious expression; it is also the sign of an identification of himself in the idealized father image in which the passive, victimized son meets with the aggressive, sensual father.

Simultaneously with the exposure of the father and his absolution by confession, Lawrence arraigns the mother in the story "Odour of Chrysanthemums." Technically the story is like "The Christening"; there is a clumsily explicit, yet lyrical insight on the woman's part, after the real action has receded. But the real sympathy here, as in "The Christening," lies with the dead father. As she looks at the body of the dead collier, she absolves him as Gertrude Morel is never capable of doing: "He was no more responsible than she. . . . 'I have been fighting a husband who did not exist. *He* existed all the time. What wrong have I done? What was that I have been living with? There lies the reality, this man.'—"[20]

The sympathy in both these stories is with the dead or the dying. In the sense that the aged collier and the dead one are the beginnings of the idealized father, the artist would appear to be embarrassed with the too particular image of his real father, and to be hurrying him off to his apotheosis. I have called the relationship with the father in this first phase an *entente cordiale;* one of its limitations on the father's independent existence is that he cannot survive as a hardy, separate identity. But this is, as Freud suggests, a knife that cuts two ways, for neither can the son, in his identification as son, survive his father's debilitation. It is again the problem of "protecting Laius." "The Shades of Spring," which deals with the two remaining principals of *Sons and Lovers,* Miriam Leivers and Paul Morel, defines the problem. John Syson is Paul Morel returning from the town where he has found his life as an artist and as a husband. His purpose in returning is to see Hilda Millership, the girl he left behind him, a girl close in every particular to the Miriam of *Sons and Lovers.* A gamekeeper confronts him, Arthur Pilbeam, Hilda's lover:

> It was a young man of four or five and twenty, ruddy and well favored. His dark blue eyes now stared aggressively at the intruder. His black moustache, very thick, was cropped short over a small rather soft mouth. In every other respect the fellow was manly and good looking . . . taut with animal life.[21]

We have met this face before in Walter Morel. We have also met the gamekeeper in *The White Peacock,* the brutal Annable. E. T. describes the real meeting Lawrence had with a gamekeeper:

> Lawrence's extraordinary obsession with gamekeepers is difficult to account for. The only encounter with a gamekeeper that occurred during the years of my acquaintance with him took place when he was a youth of seventeen. A party of us . . . penetrated unwittingly into a private portion of the Annesley Woods. . . . Suddenly a burly red-haired keeper with a youth close on his heels burst through the trees. He took my eldest brother and Lawrence aside and made them give their names. . . . We trooped home crestfallen, Lawrence white-faced and still.[22]

In *The White Peacock* the rather priggish prototype of Paul Morel, Cyril, after such a scene with Annable, befriends him, and the two preserve an uneasy friendship until Annable is killed. Like Walter Morel, Annable is exhibitionistically uncouth and goes out of his way to offend the somewhat effeminate Cyril. The complementary roles of the aggressive, brutal father and the refined, submissive son roughly anticipate their elaboration in *Sons and Lovers*. Annable is like a "devil of the woods," reminiscent of the medieval "wild man of the woods":

> "Be a good animal, true to your animal instinct," was his motto. . . . He treated me as an affectionate father treats a delicate son; I noticed he liked to put his hand on my shoulder or my knee as we talked; yet, withal he asked me questions, and saved his thoughts to tell me and believed in my knowledge like any acolyte.[23]

The features of Arthur Pilbeam are those of Walter Morel, whose own appearance derives, as E. T. points out, from Lawrence's father, Arthur Lawrence. When these features are combined in the person of a gamekeeper, with whom Lawrence's ur-experience was a frightening and humiliating brush with authority, we can account for the "extraordinary obsession" of Lawrence with gamekeepers.

The gamekeeper serves excellently as father image, sharing as he does with kings, queens, policemen, and Prussian officers the absolutist characteristics of the parent symbol. And Lawrence's gamekeeper is remarkably apt as an addition to this assemblage. He is, like Lawrence's own father, at once underling and authority, and he emerges from the poaching tradition of the Midlands. He carries a gun and protects woods and game, both of these activities, combined with the jealous conservation implicit in them, identified with sexuality and the genitals. As a father image the gamekeeper must be submitted to, or appeased, or destroyed. In *The White Peacock* Cyril submits to and appeases the gamekeeper, Annable. Whatever latent hostility there is discharges itself when this gamekeeper is destroyed in an accident. The return of the young gamekeeper, Arthur Pilbeam, involves a further aspect touched upon earlier—that of sexual rivalry, which persists in the son's relationships with other men where women are concerned. The inevitable tenderness that tempers such a rivalry shows itself. When Syson has left Pilbeam he has a compassionate afterthought for this rustic who is intellectually so inferior to him: " 'Ah, well,' he said to himself; 'the poor devil seems to have a grudge against me. I'll do my best for him.' He grinned to himself, in a very bad temper."[24]

In *Sons and Lovers* Miriam is a static figure; she is the Ophelia, the virginal side of the maternal image. In "The Shades of Spring" she undergoes a striking and significant metastasis, whose determinant is her having taken Arthur Pilbeam for a lover. Syson, in the beginning, patronizes the gamekeeper, and then he attempts to patronize Hilda, affecting an urbane admiration for her Arcadian simplicity, her nunlike innocence. But Hilda shakes his self-assurance; he is impressed by her womanliness, and by a quality in her which Lawrence contents himself by calling "static." It grows upon him that she has not changed but that she "was not what he had known her to be." "He felt himself shrinking. With an effort he kept up the ironic manner." She goes on to tell him that she had taken Pilbeam as a lover on the same night Syson had married. Syson's reaction is one of pain, out of which flows a stream of reproach that could more readily be directed at Gertrude Morel. Syson gives it as the reason for their separation:

> "You wanted me to rise in the world. And all the time you were sending me away from you—every new success of mine put a separation between us, and more for you than for me. You never wanted to come with me: you wanted just to send me to see what it was like. I believe you even wanted me to marry a lady. You wanted to triumph over society in me."[25]

Like Lydia Beardsall Lawrence, Gertrude Morel was ambitious for her sons. She wanted them to marry "girls in a better station of life." Syson's complaint seems hardly the complaint of a lover; it is more that of a child who has willy-nilly been thrust into the world. "I distinguished myself to satisfy you," need only become a cry of pain when growth and distinction make separation inevitable—the situation that must prevail when a son can no longer stop with his mother. And Hilda's reply—" 'Ah!' she cried, 'you always wanted change, change, like a child' "—suggests the latent content of the interview.

The latent identity of Hilda Millership differs from that of Miriam in one important respect: whereas in *Sons and Lovers* her sexual inviolability preserved Miriam as the virginal aspect of the mother, Hilda's becoming the mistress of a man who exhibits paternal characteristics makes possible a more advanced stage of recognition. Hilda's "fall" is accepted, although not without dismay, by Arthur Syson, and Lawrence's image of the nun—addressed first to Jessie Chambers and subsequently to Miriam—is extended to include Hilda: "He was startled to see his young love, his nun, his Botticelli angel, so revealed. It was he who had been the fool. He and she were more separate than any two strangers could be."[26]

As in "The Christening" and "Odour of Chrysanthemums," there is a greater maturity evidenced in the conscious grasp of the action of "The Shades of Spring," and with it a corresponding maturity in the unconscious motivations of the story. The nun does not become the harlot, the degraded woman who must be rescued, like Clara of *Sons and Lovers*. Syson "shrinks" under his own recognition of her as a woman, but he has now come to see her from his own autonomous career in London and his own marriage, which has coincided with Hilda's "marriage" to the gamekeeper. In *Sons and Lovers* Paul Morel returns Clara to Baxter Dawes only after he himself has possessed her sexually, and his act of renunciation is a futile attempt to recreate the parental situation which his mother's death has destroyed. But Syson has never possessed Hilda, and, if arrogantly, has released her to her proper mate.

"The Shades of Spring" ends in Syson's realization that

the woman, Hilda, is stronger than either Pilbeam, whom she describes as "thoughtful—but not beyond a certain point," or himself, intellectually superior, but the imperfect animal. It is, like the other two stories, an indictment of the woman, the mother, and an attempt to resolve the conflict between father and son. "The Shades of Spring" is a declaration of war by Lawrence against his own nature as the thought-tormented hostile son, and, beyond this, a recognition of the intellectual limitations of the father which qualify his attractive and enviable sexual potency. For "The Shades of Spring" says in effect that there must be an alliance between father and son—the identification with an idealized image compatible to both—or both will fall.

In 1912 (the story is posthumously published and the date and circumstances of composition are uncertain) Lawrence wrote a story called "The Old Adam."[27] In the characters of Mr. and Mrs. Thomas, Lawrence would seem, in part at least, to have incorporated his first impressions of the Weekleys—Ernest Weekley and his wife Frieda, with whom Lawrence was subsequently to elope. And the young man, Edward Severn, recalls Frieda's first impression of Lawrence. Harry Thornton Moore, in his biography of Lawrence, quotes Frieda Weekley's recollection of Lawrence: ". . . a long, thin figure, quick, straight legs, light, sure movements. He seeemed so obviously simple. Yet he arrested my attention. What kind of a bird was this?"[28]

Lawrence at this time was about twenty-seven years old, Frieda, thirty-four. The amplitudes of body and voice and intellect and her Continental self-assurance attracted him. Her aristocratic pedigree impressed him. And he also noted, Moore observes, that "she paid little attention to her husband."

"The Old Adam," read within the biographical context, becomes the "family romance" par excellence. The young man, Edward Severn, is a boarder in the Thomases' house.

He is "tall, and thin, but graceful in his energy. . . . He was one of those who attract by their movement, whose movement is watched unconsciously. . . . When in repose, he had the diffident, ironic bearing, so remarkable in the educated youth of today."[29]

It is about to storm; the husband is not yet home. He is described as being "something in the law." Severn and Mrs. Thomas, Gertrude, holding one of her children, are alone together. Mrs. Thomas is thirty-four, "full-bosomed and ripe. She had dark hair that twined lightly round her low, white brow."

There is an excitement between them, which Lawrence with great deftness renders obliquely:

> Mrs. Thomas watched his fine mouth lifted for kissing. She leaned forward, lowering the baby, and suddenly by a quick change in his eyes, she knew he was aware of the heavy woman's breasts approaching down to him. The wild rogue of a baby bent her face to his, and then instead of kissing him, suddenly licked his cheek with her soft wet tongue.[30]

As Severn waits with her in the half-light while the lightning flashes, their inchoate feelings perfect and recognize themselves: "Yet, time after time, as the flashes came, they looked at each other, till in the end they were both panting, and afraid, not of the lightning but of themselves and each other."[31]

About Severn's feelings Lawrence is meticulously accurate, far beyond the demands of the context. In *Sons and Lovers*, as we saw above, he had accounted for Paul Morel's chastity in these terms:

> Being the sons of mothers whose husbands had blundered rather brutally through their feminine sanctities they were themselves too diffident and shy. They could easier deny themselves than incur any reproach from a woman; for a woman was like their mother, and they were full of the sense of the mother.[32]

In "The Old Adam" the problem is restated:

> At twenty-seven he was quite chaste. Being highly civilized, he prized women for their intuition, and because of the delicacy with which he could transfer to them his thoughts and feelings, without cumbrous argument. From this to a state of passion he could only proceed by fine gradations and such a procedure he had never begun. Now he was startled, astonished, perturbed yet still scarcely conscious of his whereabouts. There was a pain in his chest that made him pant, and an involuntary tension in his arms, as if he must press someone to his breast. But the idea that this someone was Mrs. Thomas would have shocked him too much had he formed it.[33]

Ferenczi, it might be noted in connection with the "delicacy with which he could transfer to them his thoughts and feelings," describes the "dialogues of the unconscious" that take place between mother and son when the son still harbors an unconscious incestuous mother fixation. Ferenczi's example, the son's renunciation of his deep masculine voice and his raising of it to prevent the forbidden incest,[34] is apposite to Jesse Chambers' description of Lawrence's high-pitched voice, "clearly an unconscious imitation of his mother's."[35]

Mrs. Thomas' husband interrupts the breathless idyl between his wife and Severn. Here, as elsewhere in Lawrence, one of those "dialogues of the unconscious" takes place. The men are immediately hostile.

> Thomas came in, flushed very red. He was of middle stature, a thickly built man of forty, good-looking. But he had grown round shouldered with thrusting forward his chin in order to look the aggressive, strong-jawed man. . . .
>
> He did not speak to Severn nor Severn to him. Although as a rule the two men were very friendly, there came these times, when, for no reason whatever, they were sullenly hostile. Thomas sat down heavily, and reached his bottle of beer. His hands were thick, and in their movements rudi-

mentary. Severn watched the thick fingers grasp the drinking-glass as if it were a treacherous enemy.[36]

A similar situation in *Sons and Lovers* may perhaps suggest a basis for this unreasonable hostility in the more intimate context of the scene as Lawrence stages it in the novel. There are several scenes in the novel in which Walter Morel is the intruder into the closed relationship between Paul and his mother. Walter Morel's "At your mischief again," when he interrupts an exchange of tenderness between Paul and Gertrude Morel, sums up more explicitly than Thomas' sullen hostility the father's jealousy of the successful Oedipal compact betweeen mother and son. Walter Morel is the prototype for characters like Thomas. Mrs. Thomas goads the young man on to defeat her slower-witted husband in argument. She sides with her husband to encompass his downfall. "The irony of her part was delicious to her. If she had sided with Severn, the young man would have pitied the forlorn man and been gentle with him."[37]

The two men must carry a heavy box down a flight of stairs. Severn, who is described as unconsciously loving the risk involved in Thomas' being below the heavy box as they round the turn in the stairs, slips and drops his end of the box. The accident sends the older man flying.

> "You ———, you did it on purpose!" he shouted, and straightway he fetched the young man two heavy blows, upon the jaw and ear. . . . The young man had never been struck in the face before. He instantly went white and mad with rage. Thomas stood on guard, fists up. . . . With open, stiff fingers, the young man sprang on his adversary. In spite of the blow he received, but did not feel, he flung himself again forward, and then, catching Thomas' collar, brought him down with a crash. Instantly his exquisite hands were dug into the other's thick throat, the linen collar having been torn open. Thomas fought madly, with blind, brute strength. But the other lay wrapped on him like a white steel, his rare intelligence con-

centrated, not scattered; concentrated on strangling Thomas swiftly. He pressed forward, forcing his landlord's head over the edge of the next flight of stairs. Thomas, stout and full-blooded, lost every trace of self possession; he struggled like an animal at slaughter. The blood came out of his nose over his face.[38]

We are now in a position to predict the aftermath of the struggle. Severn is "wild with shame. . . . The young man's heart filled with remorse and grief. He put his arms around the heavy man and raised him, saying tenderly: 'Let me help you up.' " Mrs. Thomas, forgotten in the third corner of the triangle, watches the two men cementing their friendship in blood and gives herself over to despair: "She must no longer allow herself to hope for anything for herself. The rest of her life must be spent in self-abnegation; she must seek for no sympathy, must ask for no grace in love, no grace and harmony in living."[39] Now that he has returned, in effect, Mrs. Thomas to her husband, Severn's real "romance" is with Mr. Thomas. They grasp hands. "To the end of their acquaintance, Severn and Thomas were close friends, with a gentleness in their bearing, one towards the other. On the other hand, Mrs. Thomas was only polite and formal with Severn, treating him as if he were a stranger."[40]

In *Sons and Lovers* we found Paul Morel performing the same restitutive act following murderous violence with Baxter Dawes. There I described it as the counter-Oedipal act, the retreat from self-assertive masculinity into the fine power that virginal renunciation asserts over the sexually committed. Paul Morel lapses back into his old filial role.

I should like to overdetermine the identification of Paul Morel and Severn with Lawrence, and subsequently with the characters and actions of "The Prussian Officer," by referring to some of the elements in still another story in this collection. The story is "The Daughters of the Vicar," written, like the others, in the years 1911–12. Certain elements in the story are drawn from the same biographical data to be found, almost undisguised, in *Sons and Lovers*. The mother, Mrs. Durant, dies of the same malignant tumor that Mrs. Morel conceals until it is too late. Her relationship with her son is identical: "There was about her, too, that masterful *aplomb* of a woman who has brought up and ruled her sons; but even them she had ruled unwillingly. . . . Only she had loved her youngest boy, because he was her last, and she saw herself free."[41]

The son's response is also identical with Paul Morel's, as, indeed, is his whole personality. Alfred Durant and Paul Morel are interchangeable. "But still he remained constant to her. His feeling for her was deep and unexpressed. He noticed when she was tired, or when she had a new cap. And he bought little things for her occasionally. She was not wise enough to see how much he lived by her."[42] When she dies, "it seemed as if life in him had burst its bounds, and he was lost in a great bewildering flood, immense and unpeopled. He himself was broken and spilled out amid it all. He could only breathe panting in silence. . . . Without knowing it, he had been centralized, polarized, in his mother."[43]

> He was almost quite chaste. A strong sensitiveness had kept him from women. Sexual talk was all very well among men, but somehow it had no application to living women. There were two things for him, the *idea* of women, with which he sometimes debauched himself, and real women, before whom he felt a deep uneasiness, and a need to draw away. . . .
> . . . when the ready woman presented herself, the very fact that she was a palpable woman made it impossible for him to touch her. And this incapacity was like a core of rottenness in him.
> So several times he went, drunk, with his companions, to the licensed prostitute houses abroad. But the sordid insignificance of the experience appalled him.[44]

But several noteworthy distortions appear in "The Daughters of the Vicar." D. H. Lawrence's father, Arthur, was a miner who married the socially and intellectually superior Lydia Beardsall, whose father, George Beardsall, "was a noted preacher who often took over the Wesleyan pulpit."[45] Lawrence's father survived his wife's death by a dozen years. In "The Daughters of the Vicar" Lawrence seems to have built onto his parental history a situation in which he himself played the filial role. As Alfred Durant he recreates his father's marriage to his mother by making the young miner marry one of the vicar's daughters, Louisa. He does not, however, at the same time, abandon the character Paul Morel; the record of the mother's death and the son's chastity attest to that.

The death of Alfred Durant's father takes place almost in order that Lawrence may bring into being this significant hybrid. The son now stands in biographical apposition to the father, although in terms of their characters they are profoundly divided. Paul Morel yearns toward the lower classes who are the repository of "life itself," and likewise Alfred Durant, unhappily chaste, envies the miners:

> He would have changed with any mere brute, just to be free of himself, to be free of this shame of self-consciousness. He saw some collier lurching straight forward without misgiving, pursuing his own satisfactions, and he envied him. Anything, he would have given anything for this spontaneity and this blind stupidity which went to its own satisfaction direct.[46]

We are aware here that a significant realignment is taking place in Lawrence's protagonist—at a time anterior to *Sons and Lovers* but providing us with a tenuous anticipation of a process by which Lawrence was later to reconcile son with father. Here begins an identification, but it is merely an identification of interests and situation.

In "The Old Adam" and *Sons and Lovers* the scenes of violence between older and younger men take place between what may be called pure strains of father and son images.

The invariable outcome of these struggles, whose cause is an older woman, the wife of the older man, is the submission of the younger man and a gesture of restitution which involves the return of the woman to her rightful husband. I have described this action as a working out of the counter-Oedipal situation, in which castration is voluntarily accepted as the price of aggression, on the son's part. In these two stories the son retains the characteristics of the son who has accepted castration and identified himself with the mother, and who, although he attacks the hostile father, at the last submits to the sadomasochistic desire to be beaten by the father.

In "The Daughters of the Vicar" the son, Alfred Durant, still retains his personality as the autobiographical son, but he is mechanically transposed into a role that belongs properly to the father, that of the miner who marries the daughter of a clergyman. We encounter here not the son's wish to submit to the father, but the son's explicit wish to be like his father, "to be free of this shame of self-consciousness" and to attain "this spontaneity and this blind stupidity which went to its own satisfaction direct." We know from the premium Lawrence puts, throughout his work, on mindlessness and animal spontaneity that he is asserting against the claims of his own egohood an unrealizable ego ideal that most resembles an image of a father purged of his brutality.

Side by side with the attempt to be like the father, however, runs the residual homoerotism that survives from the earlier Oedipal situation. It expresses itself in these stories as a disguised form of sexual relationship between two men, the sadistic beating and retaliation by strangling that we have seen occur in three separate instances. The women in *Sons and Lovers* and "The Old Adam" are in the final analysis merely catalysts to the unions of the men, and in "The Prussian Officer" the nature of the relationship is frankly undisguised. If the sensuous description of the young man strangling the older and the tender aftermath were not enough to warrant our calling these encounters sexual in their natures, Havelock Ellis adds an interesting note to the act of strangling, or being strangled:

> I allude to the impulse to strangle the object of sexual desire and to the corresponding craving to be strangled. . . . Not only is the idea attractive, but, as a matter of fact, strangulation, suffocation, or any arrest of respiration, even when carried to the extent of producing death, may actually provoke emission. . . . Strangulation is the extreme and most decided type of this group of imagined or real situations in all of which respiratory disturbance seems to be an essential element.[47]

"The Prussian Officer" contains most of the elements observable in *Sons and Lovers*, "The Old Adam," and "Daughters of the Vicar." When we return to it we realize the extent to which this objective picture of Prussian militarism emerges from material with which *Sons and Lovers* has made us familiar. Like Dawes and Paul Morel, the officer and his orderly act out the phantasy of physical abuse and degradation followed by the retaliation of the younger man. But there is a significant double change in the nature of the characters and in the outcome of the struggle.

Severn, Paul Morel, and Alfred Durant, the young sons of their respective stories, are uniformly chaste, sensitive, and attached to their mothers. We should naturally expect (not that fiction should be predictable to be good) that the young orderly in "The Prussian Officer" would fall into this class, since in other respects his role is similar. And we should likewise expect that the officer would have nothing at all in common with these men.

But the reverse is true: the orderly, with his "dark expressionless eyes that seemed never to have thought, only to have received life direct through the senses and acted straight from instinct," is more like the father than he is like Paul

Morel or Alfred Durant or Severn. The officer, on the other hand, is more like Paul Morel or Alfred Durant. Between "going drunk to the licensed prostitute houses abroad" and being "appalled by the sordid insignificance of the experience," and "taking a mistress and returning dissatisfied," there lies only a social refinement of the same experience, from Alfred Durant to a Prussian aristocrat.

"The Prussian Officer" accomplishes what *Sons and Lovers* and "The Old Adam" swerve from accomplishing. It allows the homoerotism, which Lawrence has not hitherto explored, to have full sway, to realize itself in the tormented personality of the officer and the submission of the orderly and in the completed pattern of sadistic cruelty, masochistic yielding, and pleasurable retaliation. The relationship between the two men emerges as what I must make bold to call a love relationship in which the strangulation appears as the abnormal substitute for what cannot possibly become normal sexual aims. In "The Prussian Officer" the aims are recognized completely as homosexual without the specious introduction of a woman as the *casus belli*. As the officer thinks when he is alone with the orderly, "This was to be man to man with them." Not that the woman in Lawrence's life and work is a negligible factor; on the contrary. It is simply that in "The Prussian Officer" the father is having his crowded hour.

Sandor Ferenczi discriminates between the "subject-homo-erotic" and the "object-homo-erotic" as representing two distinct types of homosexuality. The first has a better time of things, unequivocally resigning his masculinity in favor of the passive, feminine role. It is the second whose life is a prolonged torment, whose repressed phantasies manifest themselves in obsessive substitutes, aggressive heterosexual activity which leaves him dissatisfied, and relationships with men in which overt object love cannot tell its name.[48]

The earliest history of the "object-homo-erotic" reveals

"a true neurotic compulsion, with logically irreversible substitutes of normal sexual aims and actions by abnormal ones."[49]
In short, he shows the typical heterosexual tendencies in
his Oedipal phantasies, i.e., "sexual-sadistic plans of assault
on the mother (or her representative) and cruel death-wishes
against the disturbing father. Further, they were all intellectually precocious."[50] These "normal" aims are deflected to
the abnormal homoerotic aims usually as the result of a
prohibition (not necessarily a verbal one) delivered by either
parent regarding the child's heterosexual activity. What
ensues from the prohibition is an obstinate, anxiety-attended,
obsessive turning to homoerotic activity.

But the original aim is not lost: "It turns out that an
object-homo-erotic knows how to love the woman in a man;
the posterior half of a man's body can signify for him the
anterior half of a woman's. . . ."[51] The man is merely a substitute for the normal heterosexual object.

> In the light of psycho-analysis, therefore, the active homo-
> erotic act appears on the one hand as subsequent (false) obedi-
> ence, which—taking the parental interdiction literally—really
> avoids intercourse with women, but indulges the forbidden
> homo-erotic desires in unconscious phantasies; on the other
> hand the paederastic act serves the purpose of the original
> Oedipus phantasy [to injure the father] and denotes the injur-
> ing and sullying of the man. . . .
>
> The homo-erotic obsessional idea unites in a happy com-
> promise the flight from women, and their symbolic replace-
> ment, as well as the hatred of men and the compensation of
> this. Woman being apparently excluded from the love-life,
> *there no longer exists so far as consciousness is concerned, any*
> *bone of contention between father and son* [italics mine].[52]

Sons and Lovers would confirm our hypothesizing some
such psychic background for its genesis. But the manifest
homoerotic component is absent except as it exhibits itself
in the incomplete struggle between Paul Morel and Baxter

Dawes in their plausible rivalry over the woman. In "The Prussian Officer," however, this component emerges completely; we are dealing with material that, because it is art and not symptom formation, must be regarded as controlled phantasy. In this story Lawrence has worked through what in *Sons and Lovers* he was tending toward, a realignment of identities, which in Lawrence's own life could only remain a passionate yearning. The orderly is, by virtue of his youth and subordination, the son, but he is also, by virtue of his healthy, instinctual nature and physique, a fusion of ego ideal as it identifies itself with the good father image. He does not relinquish his role as the oppressed victim, or his retaliation against the brutal older man, as Morel and Severn do.

But the son also realizes another wish, the wish to *become* the brutal father, to be the aggressor, to torment as he has been tormented, to perform the act "whose unconscious aim is revenge upon the father."

Out of this mingling of personalities there emerge two significant hybrids, the one combining within himself the good aspects of the father, the other, all the hated attributes of both father and son. Hero and antihero, self and antiself face one another.

In the captain we find isolated and rejected that side of himself Lawrence sought to repudiate, the hypersensitive, "cerebral," sexually inhibited, mother-dominated son—the Cyrils, Paul Morels, Alfred Durants, Severns, Sysons, and Clifford Chatterleys of the stories and novels. The new figure, the orderly, does not turn back from the strangling of this captain. The "scruple of love and fear" does not lead him to flight from manhood; and the masochistic impulse to submit appears only as a residue—a morbid but tender solicitude for the broken body of the older man. In their death struggle Lawrence divests himself in a work of art of a primordial phantasy. It stands as a memorandum to the ego he created for himself that love of the father is the ground of its being.

It should not surprise us at this point that Lawrence has found his way with the prophetic blindness of Oedipus himself through the singular experience of his own life to what, as "The Prussian Officer," becomes a public, universal assertion.

I have described *Sons and Lovers* as a meridian from which to measure Lawrence's development as man and artist. "The Prussian Officer" provides us with a unifying psychological principle for determining the direction of that development, which by and large consisted of his search for a protagonist and a philosophy that could best express these filial-paternal strains. The way to such a reconciliation, in Lawrence's case, was inevitably beset with difficulties, involving the fine balance of antipathy with identification and love with fear and hatred. The artist is barely afloat in the caldron of ambivalence. The Prussian orderly can only point.

The years 1911-13 were crucial years in Lawrence's life; they saw his mother's death, and the publication of his first novels, *The White Peacock, The Trespasser,* and *Sons and Lovers.* They saw his flight with Frieda Weekley. We must bear in mind as we read these early stories of fierce, murderous struggles between unequally matched men, the deaths of mothers, and the sudden sexual attractions between men and women, that Lawrence in his own life was pursuing similar adventures and suffering a real bereavement. There is an important correlation between his life and his art, of which his art is the chronicle.

The end of *Sons and Lovers* describes Paul Morel forced to a choice between a dead mother and the lights of the living town, between the "drift toward death" and life, the *thanatos* and the *eros* instincts. The one implies a lapse into the permanent role of the unproductive, bereaved son; the other, the assumption of a new role, the aggressive, productive husband. Paul Morel walks toward the town.

It is unfortunate for Lawrence, as indeed it is for any artist, that his nature cannot imitate his art, so that with the esthetically satisfying resolution of his novel there could also take place the psychologically satisfying resolution of his neurosis. *Sons and Lovers* and "The Prussian Officer" as works of art are, so to speak, the imitations of a release from the Oedipal ties. They imply not so much a rejection of the mother as the life-saving impulse on Lawrence's part to throw his lot in with the father—the aggressive, virile principle that could allow him in a moment to become artist, husband, no longer son. In his life in the world, Lawrence, like James Joyce at the conclusion of *A Portrait of the Artist as a Young Man*, calls not upon his mother but upon his father to "stand him now and ever in good stead."

What Lawrence's works will demonstrate from this point forward, with almost mathematical economy, are the steps by which the elemental situation of *Sons and Lovers* transformed itself into its polar opposite.

As a corollary to the repressed, unappeased homoerotic sexual aims in the modern man, Ferenczi describes the displacement of this "sexual hunger" to an abnormal dedication to heterosexual drives. "I quite seriously believe that the men of today are one and all obsessively heterosexual as the result of this affective displacement; in order to free themselves from men, they become the slaves of women."[53]

Lawrence's acknowledgment of this slavery, to the extent that he could be objective about it, is explicit in a letter he wrote to Katherine Mansfield, a letter in which his friend John Middleton Murry figures, as he will figure in *Women in Love*, as a whipping boy for Lawrence. The date is 1918.

> I send you the Jung book. . . . Beware of it—this mother-incest idea can become an obsession. But it seems to me there is this much truth in it; that at certain periods the man has a desire and a tendency to return unto the woman, make her his goal and his end, find his justification in her. In this way he casts himself as it were into her womb, and she, the Magna Mater, receives him with gratification. This is a kind of incest. It seems to me it is what Jack does to you, and what repels and fascinates you. I have done it, and now struggle with all my might to get out. In a way Frieda is the devouring mother. . . . But Frieda says I am antediluvian in my positive attitude. I do think a woman must yield some sort of precedence to a man, and he must take this precedence. I do think men must go ahead absolutely in front of their women, without turning around to ask for permission or approval from their women. Consequently the women must follow as it were unquestioningly.[54]

The Jung book is undoubtedly *The Psychology of the Unconscious*, translated in 1916. Chapter vi, "The Battle for Deliverance from the Mother," must have riven Lawrence's prophetic soul with its appositeness to his own situation. Two things strike us in this letter to Katherine Mansfield: one is his now almost calm acceptance, via Jung, of the devouring mother image; the other is his strenuous orientation, already noted in "The Prussian Officer," but now in connection with his own marriage, toward the father's less sensitive, more masterful attitude toward women. A certain pathos breathes through the letter; Lawrence's walking in front of his woman sounds more like a program than a natural gesture. But it perpetuates at least the outward forms that Lawrence described when he wrote about Nottinghamshire coal miners walking out with their wives and cronies on a day off.

In his attempts to exorcise the Ave Maria of *Sons and Lovers* from his work, Lawrence, the artist, practiced continual gemination upon himself. He consigns his hyper-intellectual, hypersensitive personality at times to the spokesman for his cultus, from whence he sings the mindless man from the top of his intellect, or else to the enemies of instinct, the Gerald Criches and Clifford Chatterleys. His other self, patterned after the father ideal, he fashions into the gamekeepers, miners, and artisans.

The marvelous fortuity that made Lawrence's extempore marriage to Frieda Weekley a final relationship owes its permanence to the fact that, in addition to her intrinsic beauty and intelligence, her situation was designed to be irresistibly appealing to him. Like Clara Dawes in *Sons and Lovers*, she has described herself as having been, until Lawrence's advent, "unawakened." Older than Lawrence, with three children, with none of the restraints associated with the "woman of impeccable moral purity," married to a man who was bound to be "injured" and who, moreover, stood, as Lawrence's professor, *in loco parentis*, she fulfills, like a fairy-tale princess, an extraordinary array of conditions. Even her social status, superior to Lawrence's, provided a distorted recapitulation of the marriage of Lawrence's well-bred mother to an underbred miner. In all these instances, Lawrence, so far as his art was concerned, was making autobiographical points around which his ideas could rally.

It is not that his life relates to his writing in a *post hoc ergo propter hoc* sense, but that the same unconscious sources fed both the actions of his fiction and the events of his life. His marriage as a totality of conscious and unconscious motivations was to provide Lawrence with the physical body of his symbolism. The miners of *Sons and Lovers* now forsake their naturalistic degradation to become the dark, underground, threatening, sensual male principle. And the well-bred lady, the bourgeois mother of *Sons and Lovers*, becomes the passive, unawakened female principle, whose perceptions the man must waken. It is as if, with extraordinary luck, Oedipus had fled from Thebes to Corinth to marry his foster mother Merope.

In his flight from his filial bondage Lawrence was trying to escape "the grey disease," as he called it, of mental consciousness. The imagery in which he envelops it, as for example in criticizing Marcel Proust, involves masturbation, which, like Swift's scatology, aroused his ultimate disgust. I equate Lawrence's rejection of mental consciousness with his rejection of his old incest fixation on his mother. The object of the original masturbation phantasy is, Freud insists, the mother herself. For Lawrence, in sexual relations an understanding between minds constituted a very real incest, implicit in the act of *knowing* someone sexually. To the psychologist, Dr. Trigant Burrow, Lawrence wrote:

> Do you know somebody who said: *on connait les femmes, ou on les aime; il n'y a pas de milieu?* It's French, but I'm not sure it isn't true. I'm not sure if a mental relation with a woman doesn't make it impossible to love her. To know the *mind* of a woman is to end in hating her. Love means the pre-cognitive flow—neither strictly has a mind—It is the honest state before the apple.[55]

He provides, for the puritan temperament, a handbook for sinners. In *Women in Love*, for example, the characters of Gerald Crich and Gudrun are the more terrible for representing to him the forcibly controlled desires of his own psyche. There lies between them, as he puts it, an "obscene recognition," and he flies from it into synthetic yogic philosophies and cultural primitivism. It is a flight from the mother in the mind to the father in the blood.

Lawrence Durrell, in his novel *Balthazar*, has one of his characters describe Lawrence as a man with a "habit of building a Taj Mahal around anything as simple as a good f——k."[56] Nothing could be further from the truth. The same unconscious processes we have described in other contexts manifest themselves here as well.

The sexual descriptions in Lawrence's novels contain always the imagery of what is recognizable as coitus anxiety, which implies a neurotic regression to some prior state, before the genitals have assumed primacy as the sexual organ par excellence, when for the child the pleasurable organ is the mouth, which does not give but receives through suckling. The orally dependent infant, for whom all orifices in phantasy satisfy oral (sucking) needs, fears the giving of himself in an orgasm. His own hunger, which he attributes as well to the object of his desire, the nursing mother, threatens to devour him. The neurotic Oedipal man, for whom the nursing situation was the paradisal one, equates orgasm with loss and withdraws in horror from a mother image that is more predator than nurse. The clinical descriptions are consistently those of death; violent, explosive annihilation; and mutilation.[57]

Lawrence explores the full octave of this experience, from violent, prolonged, torment on the edge of orgasm to complete annihilation and nirvana. But bliss is never certain. In his novel *The Rainbow*, which, like Mann's *Buddenbrooks*, crosses through three generations, Lawrence takes up the marriage of Will and Anna Brangwen and finally the relationship between the daughter, Ursula, and her lover Skrebensky. In both we are aware of both the desire for, and the dread of, coitus. We are aware also of the tremendous overvaluation of the woman and the unconscious incestuous content latent in it, manifesting itself in the pleasurable intellectual experience of shame, which in *The Rainbow* is almost Byronic in its unabashed intensity.

That the experiences represent Lawrence's could be deduced from his repeated and idiosyncratic handling of them, experiences so personal as to be unique, even if we doubted Frieda Lawrence's statement that the "inner relationship [between Ursula and Skrebensky] is Lawrence's and mine."[58] The first relationship is between Anna and Will Brangwen:

He [Brangwen] had always all his life had a secret dread of Absolute Beauty. It had always been like a fetish to him, something to fear, really, for it was immoral and against mankind. . . . But now he had given way, and with infinite sensual violence gave himself to the realization of this supreme, immoral Absolute Beauty in the body of a woman. . . .

But still the thing terrified him. Awful and theatening it was, dangerous to a degree, even whilst he gave himself to it. . . . All the shameful natural and unnatural acts of sensual voluptuousness which he and the woman partook of together, created together, they had their heavy beauty and their delight. Shame, what was it? It was part of extreme delight.[59]

In the relationship between Ursula and Skrebensky the anxieties take the upper hand, and the pleasurable sense of shame is absent. The imagery is wholly that of destruction, fear of being devoured combining with castration anxiety, a fear of the *vagina dentata* of the virgin:

His heart melted in fear from the fierce, beaked harpy's kiss. . . . The fight, the struggle for consummation was terrible. It lasted till it was agony in his soul, till he succumbed, till he gave way as if dead. . . . He felt as if the knife were being pushed into his already dead body. . . . He felt, if ever he must see her again, his bones must be broken, his body crushed, obliterated for ever. . . .

Even, in his frenzy, he sought for her mouth with his mouth, though it was like putting his face into some awful death. She yielded to him, and he pressed himself upon her in extremity, his soul groaning over and over, ["Let me come, let me come."][60]

A horrible sickness gripped him, as if his legs were really cut away and he could not move, but remained a crippled trunk, dependent, worthless. The ghastly sense of helplessness, as if he were a mere figure, that did not exist vitally, made him mad, beside himself. . . . After each contact his mad dependence on her was deepened. . . . He felt himself a mere attribute of her.[61]

Women in Love presents ostensibly two men and two women whose relationships are respectively desirable and undesirable. Gerald Crich, the blond man of power, was conceived of by Lawrence as a composite figure, derived from a mine operator in the Midlands coal regions and Lawrence's friend Middleton Murry. Gudrun, Gerald's mistress, is Katherine Mansfield.[62] The character of Rupert Birkin is presumably Lawrence himself. But if we accept this separation of identities we deny the continuity of Lawrence's self-description, and his ubiquity in sexual relationships whose common denominator is the anxiety manifested above. From Birkin's own actions we suspect that his search for "polarity" and "otherness" and the "ultraphallic" emerges from the fear of the intrauterine absorption that his friend Gerald seeks. On the strength of Gerald's actions and his resemblance to other earlier characters in Lawrence's work (the Prussian officer comes to mind), I would maintain that Gerald is psychically closer to Lawrence than Birkin—that Gerald is Lawrence's practical involvement in the world, and Birkin merely, perhaps totally, his dialectic personified.

Gerald Crich, like Paul Morel, comes to a woman for relief, Paul after his mother's death, the other after his father's. Gerald's experience is a curious mixture:

> And she [Gudrun], she was the great bath of life, he worshipped her. Mother and substance of all life she was. And he, child and man, received of her and was made whole. His pure body was almost killed, but the miraculous soft effluence of her breast suffused over him, over his seared, damaged brain, like a healing lymph, like a soft, soothing flow of life itself, perfect as if he were bathed in the womb again. . . . Like a child at the breast he cleaved intensely to her and she could not put him away.[63]

It is between Gerald and Gudrun that the obscene mental recognition of their mutual sensuality occurs, the "shame" that with Will Brangwen "was part of extreme delight." And now in this extravagant image the coitus is transformed into a nursing phantasy in which the brain, in an exotic displacement of orgastic relief, is put to sleep at the breast of the mother, the man becomes infant.

In *Aaron's Rod*, Aaron Sisson, one of Lawrence's composite selves, is sick unto death for having surrendered himself to a woman. " 'I felt it—I felt it go, inside me, the minute I gave in to her. It's perhaps killed me,' " he tells his friend Lilly.[64] Lawrence's women destroy with the power of love. They draw men to them, only to destroy them. In *Aaron's Rod* they are not beaked predators; they are constrictors.

Josephine Hay, the *belle dame* of Aaron's delirium, is an undeveloped version of the Gudrun of *Women in Love*. She is the artist woman, sexually attractive and intellectually aware. She does not fulfill herself sexually at the man's expense but is herself sexually disinherited, Lilith, not Eve. Lawrence envelops her in serpent imagery, describes her licking her "rather full, dry lips with the rapid tip of her tongue. It was an odd movement, suggesting a snake's flicker."[65]

For Lawrence, as for Yeats, there is something deathly about the woman in whom physical beauty and clarity of mind are combined. It is a confusion of genres that a beautiful woman, a silent artifact, should have opinions, destructive foibles, a will. Lawrence treats the woman artist as she appears in Josephine and Gudrun as a sexual monster. He equates the "will," that ultimate term of opprobrium when he applies it to the unsubmissive woman, with the conscious act of creation, reserving it on the physical plane for the man's aggressive phallicism and on the intellectual plane for the artist's shaping spirit. In either case the exercise of the will is the male function. In the female it becomes the harpy's beak, the snake's flicker.

In Josephine the full import of the snake is unrealized. Lawrence's maternal women, those who destroy with the power of love rather than the power of negation, are constrictors, women like Anna Brangwen, the sacred pythoness of *The Rainbow*, and Lottie of *Aaron's Rod*. With these women he dwells not on the snake's flicker but on its heavy coils, its crushed, flat look, and its tenacity:

> [Aaron] had a certain horror of her [Lottie]. The strange liquid sound of her appeal seemed to him like the swaying of a serpent which mesmerizes the fated, helpless bird. She clasped her arms around him, she drew him to her, she half roused his passion.[66]

The imagery of destruction that inheres in Lawrence's description of sexuality is a reminder of the "catastrophe theory" Ferenczi describes: "Many neurotics unconsciously regard coitus as an activity which either directly or subsequently is calculated to endanger life or limb, and in particular to damage the genital organ, i.e., an act in which are combined gratification and severe anxiety."[67] Lawrence swings continually in his novels between the nirvana imagery of "being given in peace" and the recoil from it. It is an endless cycle of Oedipal and anti-Oedipal impulses.

Even in *Lady Chatterley's Lover*, in which finally the Son of Woman is brought to bliss, the gamekeeper Mellors, in his catalogue of women, recalls to mind the harpy's beak, this time displaced below: "She sort of got harder and harder to bring off, and she'd sort of tear at me down there, as if it was a beak tearing at me."[68]

As time went on Lawrence consolidated this recoil from the orgasm into a synthetic philosophy derived mainly from yogic quietism. Thus he justified it in terms of the conservation of vital energy. *The Plumed Serpent*, Lawrence's novel about Mexico, describes the sexual relations between the Englishwoman Kate and the Indian Don Cipriano:

> When, in their love, it came back on her, the seething, electric female ecstasy, which knows such spasms of delirium, he recoiled from her. . . . By a dark and powerful instinct he drew away from her as soon as this desire rose again in her. . . . She could not know him.[69]

The character of Cipriano is perhaps a clue to the strategy Lawrence had recourse to. He belongs to the dark, mindless, instinctive order of beings with whom Lawrence identified the father. To this figure Lawrence imputed an attribute of virility which often qualifies the appeal of his protagonists —their high indifference to the woman's sexual enjoyment. It becomes increasingly more pronounced in Lawrence's later works and can only be interpreted as an unconscious equation between orgasm and annihilation or, again, between orgasm and castration. In the father there is security from the woman. The son, the server of woman, is always in danger.

It is impossible within this context to overlook the innumerable allusions in Lawrence's fiction, letters, and essays to Christ's passion, crucifixion, and resurrection—allusions that culminate, finally, in *The Man Who Died*. But, in terms of the castration anxiety that terrifies his characters, it is perhaps more in connection with the mutilations of Attis and Osiris than with Christ that the messianic theme in Lawrence becomes understandable. For Lawrence is the martyrologist of the sexual experience in all his works, from *Sons and Lovers* to *Lady Chatterley's Lover*. We have seen, in *Sons and Lovers*, how Paul Morel, in resigning from his manhood's rivalry with Baxter Dawes and returning to his childhood's dependence on his mother, achieves power over "their three fates" as the prize for his renunciation. We see, in *Lady Chatterley's Lover*, the gulf Lawrence sets between the gamekeeper and the mutilated Clifford, with his "queer, craven idolatry" of Constance and his lapse into a perverse childhood under the care of Mrs. Bolton, "the Magna Mater." We have seen throughout Lawrence's work his revulsion from the role of the "server of woman," and its agonizing alternatives. But it is not until we adopt the vantage point of *The Man Who Died* that the mythical formulation becomes clear.

On the one hand, the Jesus who survives his crucifixion reviews the life-denying tenets of his doctrine with regret. He sees himself as the dupe of his female followers, the Son of Woman, and not the Son of Man. He meets, in Mary Magdalen, the possessive, self-conscious adoration of a woman determined to grovel at the feet of a messiah who conforms to her own epicene vision. Her virtue is the virtue of the reformed prostitute who despises what she used most to enjoy. She therefore worships the ascetic Christ to the chagrin of the man in him. He has become the apotheosis of castration.

On the other hand, he accomplishes his regeneration as a man (his cry, "I am risen!" describes a phallic, synecdochic resurrection) in the arms of the priestess of Isis. Her acceptance of him is free of the mental, personal relationship he has known with Magdalen. She allows him to become the virile Christ, absolved of the recognitions so fatal to his manhood.

I read *The Man Who Died*, coming as it does so close in time to the composition of *Lady Chatterley's Lover*, as the spiritual abstract of that novel, its anagogic level made explicit. In *The Man Who Died* Lawrence has an eschatological fling at the antinatural doctrines of Christianity. In *Lady Chatterley's Lover* he extends the theme and tilts against the dark, satanic windmills of our own century's mechanistic civilization.

Clifford Chatterley, like Christ before he repudiated himself or, if you please, Attis irredeemably mutilated, is the castrate par excellence, the apotheosis of industrialism, "queer and rapacious and civilized with broad shoulders and no real legs." He is full of sage platonisms and contemptuous of the flesh. His sister-in-law, Hilda, who like Magdalen has had her lovers and destroyed them in her service, now despises sex and admires Clifford because he has none.

But it is the gamekeeper Mellors who runs the gamut

from the crucified Jesus to the coming forth by day of the phallic Osiris. He is, when he first appears, in a touch-me-not stage of resurrection, on the margin of life. Like the farmhouse in which Christ recovers, the gamekeeper's cottage lies between some spiritual Calvary and Jerusalem, between the great dead pile of Wragby Hall and the squalors of Tevershall. Constance Chatterley's coming about to an acceptance of the impersonal nature of her sexual communion with the gamekeeper as a thing indifferent to the individual communicant has its analogue in the shift from the ascetic Christ to the risen Osiris. In her complete subjection lies his peace.

↗   ↗   ↗

Lawrence's biographies are full, for the most part, of the passionate gossip of his female followers, overripe, self-important with the mysteries of self-discovery that the sexual emancipation brought with it. Endless debates take place in Lawrence's idiom on the giving up of the will, mysterious communions, "flows," and cessations of "flow," as if Lawrence's relations with women were a kind of spiritual pipeline.

Mabel Dodge Luhan, one of Lawrence's most constant admirers, offers us a significant glimpse into Lawrence's life with Frieda Lawrence:

> I saw the big voluptuous woman standing naked in the dim stone room where we dressed and undressed, and there were often great black and blue bruises on her blond flesh. . . . "I cannot stand it," she wept. "He tears me to pieces. Last night he was so loving and so tender with me, and this morning he hates me. He hit me—and said he would not be any woman's servant. Sometimes I believe he is mad!" . . . Whenever, reunited to Frieda, he capitulated to her and sank into the flesh, he beat her up for it afterwards.[70]

If *Lady Chatterley's Lover* appears to still these violent oscillations in the perfected union of the lady and the gamekeeper, it is because the novel is Lawrence's *nunc dimittis*. His physical life about to end, his writing has conjugated the verbs "love" and "hate" and declined the nouns "mother" and "father" to the perfect tense and the vocative case. *Sons and Lovers* to *Lady Chatterley's Lover* represents the full range. The shift from the parricidal Paul Morel running to his mother's arms while the father whines in the kitchen, to the "great blond child-man," Clifford Chatterley, fondling the housekeeper's breasts while the gamekeeper waits in the Park, represents the total dilapidation of Lawrence's Oedipal longings and the perfection of his reactive anti-Oedipal vision of life. Along with the heroic contempt for the mother image in absolute decay comes the full identification with the once-despised father. But for Lawrence, the man, I suspect, the shift was more apparent than real. He has merely borrowed the stones of a cathedral to build himself an obelisk.[71]

NOTES

CHAPTER I

1. Lionel Trilling, "Art and Neurosis," in *The Liberal Imagination* (New York: Doubleday and Co., 1953), p. 172.

2. T. S. Eliot, "Hamlet and His Problem" (1919), in *Selected Essays* (New York: Harcourt-Brace and Co., 1932), p. 125.

3. Sigmund Freud, "An Obsessional Neurosis," in *The Standard Edition of the Complete Psychological Works of Sigmund Freud,* translated from the German under the general editorship of James Strachey in collaboration with Anna Freud (hereafter referred to as *The Standard Edition*) (London: Hogarth Press, 1955-61), X, 175-76.

4. Ernest Jones, *The Life and Works of Sigmund Freud* (New York: Basic Books, 1959), I, 13.

5. Sandor Ferenczi, *Sex in Psychoanalysis* (*Contributions to Psychoanalysis*), authorized translation by Ernest Jones (New York: Dover Publications, 1956), pp. 234-35.

CHAPTER II

1. D. H. Lawrence, *Sons and Lovers* (New York: Harper and Brothers, 1951). Page references refer to this edition throughout.

2. Mark Schorer, "Technique as Discovery," *Hudson Review,* I (Spring, 1948), 67-87.

3. Aldous Huxley (ed.), *The Letters of D. H. Lawrence* (1st ed.; London: William Heinemann, 1932), p. 102.

4. C. G. Jung, *Psychology of the Unconscious,* translated by B. M. Hinkle (New York: Dodd, Mead and Co., 1952), p. 267.

5. E. T., *D. H. Lawrence: A Memoir* (New York: Knight, 1936), p. 191.

6. Ernest Jones, *Hamlet and Oedipus* (New York: W. W. Norton and Co., 1949), p. 122.

7. Freud, "Family Romances," in *The Standard Edition,* IX (1959), 237-41 *passim.*

8. Harry Thornton Moore, *The Life and Works of D. H. Lawrence* (New York: Twayne Publishers, 1951), p. 95.

9. *Sons and Lovers,* p. 13.

10. E. T., *D. H. Lawrence,* p. 43.

11. *Sons and Lovers,* p. 10.

12. *Ibid.,* pp. 14, 15.

13. *Ibid.,* pp. 20, 21.

14. *Ibid.,* pp. 29, 30.

15. E. T., *D. H. Lawrence,* p. 138.

16. *Sons and Lovers,* p. 34.

17. *Ibid.,* p. 34.

18. *Ibid.,* p. 136.

19. *Ibid.,* p. 146.

20. *Ibid.,* p. 253.

21. *Ibid.,* p. 251

22. Jones, *Hamlet and Oedipus,* p. 79.

23. *Ibid.,* p. 93.

24. Freud, "Dostoevsky and Parricide," in *The Standard Edition,* XXI (1961), 184-85.

25. Ernest Jones, *Hamlet and Oedipus,* p. 79.

26. *Sons and Lovers,* p. 74.

27. *Ibid.,* p. 105.

28. E. T., *D. H. Lawrence,* p. 26.

29. *Sons and Lovers,* p. 322.

30. *Ibid.*

31. *Ibid.,* p. 323.

32. *Ibid.,* p. 401.

33. *Ibid.,* p. 403.

34. *Ibid.,* p. 405.

35. *Ibid.*, p. 429.

36. *Ibid.*, p. 431.

37. *Ibid.*, p. 445.

38. *Ibid.*, p. 476.

39. Freud, "A Special Type of Choice of Object Made by Men," in *The Standard Edition*, XI (1957), 172.

40. Karl Abraham, *Clinical Papers and Essays on Psychoanalysis*, translated by Hilda Abraham (New York: Basic Books, 1955), pp. 72, 73.

CHAPTER III

1. D. H. Lawrence, *Sons and Lovers* (New York: Harper and Brothers, 1951), p. 111.

2. *Ibid.*, p. 284.

3. *Ibid.*, pp. 45, 46.

4. Sigmund Freud, "A Special Type of Choice of Object Made by Men," in *The Standard Edition*, XI (1957), 170.

5. E. T., *D. H. Lawrence: A Memoir* (New York: Knight, 1936), p. 153.

6. *Sons and Lovers*, p. 190.

7. *Ibid.*, p. 251.

8. *Ibid.*, p. 285.

9. *Ibid.*, p. 405.

10. *Ibid.*, p. 431.

11. *Ibid.*, p. 451.

12. *Ibid.*, p. 407.

13. *Ibid.*, p. 80.

14. *Ibid.*, p. 459.

15. *Ibid.*, p. 461.

16. *Ibid.*, p. 466.

17. *Ibid.*, p. 482.

18. Freud, "A Special Type of Choice of Object Made by Men," *passim*.

19. *Ibid.*, p. 168.

20. *Ibid.*, pp. 170, 171.

21. Ernest Jones, *Hamlet and Oedipus* (New York: W. W. Norton and Co., 1949), p. 85.

22. *Sons and Lovers*, p. 193.

23. *Ibid.*, p. 177.

24. *Ibid.*, p. 183.

25. *Ibid.*, p. 295.

26. E. T., *D. H. Lawrence*, p. 189.

27. Ernest Jones, *Hamlet and Oedipus*, p. 86.

28. *Sons and Lovers*, p. 186.

29. *Ibid.*, p. 254.

30. *Ibid.*, p. 170.

31. *Ibid.*, p. 328.

32. *Ibid.*, p. 257.

33. *Ibid.*, p. 338.

34. *Ibid.*, p. 337.

35. *Ibid.*, p. 376.

36. Freud, "The Taboo of Virginity," in *The Standard Edition*, XI (1957), 198–99.

37. *Sons and Lovers*, p. 269.

38. *Ibid.*, p. 294.

39. *Ibid.*, p. 326.

40. *Ibid.*, p. 332.

41. Lawrence describes this separation in a letter to Edward Garnett, describing Paul's affair with Clara: "The son decides to leave his soul in his mother's hands and, like his elder brother, go for passion" (Aldous Huxley [ed.], *The Letters of D. H. Lawrence* [1st ed.; London: William Heinemann, 1932], p. 760).

42. *Sons and Lovers*, p. 275.

43. E. T., *D. H. Lawrence*, p. 202.

44. *Sons and Lovers*, p. 275.

45. *Ibid.*, p. 221.

46. *Ibid.*, p. 308.

47. *Ibid.*, p. 317.

48. *Ibid.*, p. 389.

49. *Ibid.*, p. 415.

50. Sigmund Freud, "On the Universal Tendency to Debasement in the Sphere of Love," in *The Standard Edition*, XI (1957), 183.

51. *Sons and Lovers*, p. 427.

52. *Ibid.*, p. 366.

53. *Ibid.*, p. 145.

54. *Ibid.*, p. 32.

55. *Ibid.*, p. 68.

56. *Ibid.*, p. 160.

57. *Ibid.*, p. 251.

58. D. H. Lawrence, *Aaron's Rod* (New York: Thomas Seltzer, 1922), p. 135: "Suddenly she sprang to her feet and clutched him by the shirt-neck, her hand inside his soft collar, half strangling him. . . . His soul went black as he looked at her. He broke her hand away from his shirt collar, bursting the stud-holes."

59. *Sons and Lovers*, p. 453.

60. *Ibid.*, p. 483.

61. *Ibid.*, p. 487.

62. *Ibid.*, p. 134.

CHAPTER IV

1. Sandor Ferenczi, "The Nosology of Male Homosexuality (Homo-erotism)," in *Sex in Psychoanalysis*, translated by Ernest Jones (New York: Dover Publications, 1956), p. 74.

2. Aldous Huxley (ed.), *The Letters of D. H. Lawrence* (1st ed.; London: William Heinemann, 1932), p. 74.

3. D. H. Lawrence, "The Prussian Officer," in *The Prussian Officer* (New York: Huebsch, 1917), p. 9.

4. *Ibid.*, p. 2.

5. *Ibid.*, p. 3.

6. *Ibid.*, p. 4.

7. *Ibid.*, pp. 23–24.

8. *Ibid.*, p. 25.

9. *Ibid.*, p. 32.

10. Edward Nehls (ed.), *A Composite Biography of D. H. Lawrence* (Madison: University of Wisconsin Press, 1958), I, 106.

11. See above, pp. 16–19, *passim*.

12. See above, p. 49.

13. D. H. Lawrence, *Sons and Lovers* (New York: Harper and Brothers, 1951), p. 301.

14. See above, p. 21.

15. *Sons and Lovers*, p. 404.

16. See above, p. 32.

17. D. H. Lawrence, *The White Peacock* (Hamburg: Albatross, 1932), p. 40.

18. D. H. Lawrence, "The Christening," in *The Prussian Officer*," p. 278.

19. *Ibid.*, p. 280.

20. D. H. Lawrence, "Odour of Chrysanthemums," in *The Prussian Officer*, p. 308.

21. D. H. Lawrence, "The Shades of Spring," in *The Prussian Officer*, p. 154.

22. E. T., *D. H. Lawrence: A Memoir* (New York: Knight, 1936), p. 118.

23. *The White Peacock*, p. 161.

24. "The Shades of Spring," p. 158.

25. *Ibid.*, p. 170.

26. *Ibid.*, p. 172.

27. D. H. Lawrence, "The Old Adam," in *A Modern Lover* (London: Martin Secker, 1934).

28. Harry Thornton Moore, *The Intelligent Heart: The Story of D. H. Lawrence* (New York: Farrar, Straus and Young, 1954), p. 112. There are other contenders for these roles, and no doubt the Thomases are composites.

29. "The Old Adam," p. 47.

30. *Ibid.*, p. 53.

31. *Ibid.*, p. 58.

32. *Sons and Lovers*, p. 328.

33. "The Old Adam," p. 59.

34. Sandor Ferenczi, *Further Contributions to the Theory and Technique of Psychoanalysis*, translated by J. Suttie (London: Hogarth Press, 1926), p. 109.

35. E. T., *D. H. Lawrence*, p. 26.

36. "The Old Adam," p. 67.

37. *Ibid.*, p. 66.

38. *Ibid.*, p. 67.

39. *Ibid.*, p. 67.

40. *Ibid.*, p. 71.

41. "The Daughters of the Vicar," in *The Prussian Officer*, p. 68.

42. *Ibid.*, p. 104.

43. *Ibid.*, p. 105.

44. *Ibid.*, pp. 105–6.

45. Moore, *The Intelligent Heart*, p. 6.

46. "The Daughters of the Vicar," p. 107.

47. Havelock Ellis, *Studies in the Psychology of Sex* (Philadelphia: F. A. Davis, 1928), III, 151.

48. Ferenczi, "The Nosology of Male Homosexuality (Homo-

erotism)," pp. 250–68 *passim*.

49. *Ibid.*, p. 259.

50. *Ibid.*

51. *Ibid.*, p. 261.

52. *Ibid.*, p. 262.

53. *Ibid.*, p. 267.

54. Huxley, *The Letters of D. H. Lawrence*, p. 458.

55. *Ibid.*, p. 688.

56. Lawrence Durrell, *Balthazar* (New York: E. P. Dutton and Co., 1958), p. 114.

57. Sylvan Keiser, "Body Ego during Orgasm," *Psychoanalytic Quarterly*, XXI (April, 1952), 153–56 *passim*.

58. Moore, *The Intelligent Heart*, p. 190.

59. D. H. Lawrence, *The Rainbow* (New York: Modern Library, n.d.), p. 223.

60. *Ibid.*, p. 303. Suppressed bracketed quotation from Moore, *The Intelligent Heart*, p. 209.

61. *The Rainbow*, p. 453.

62. Nehls, *A Composite Biography of D. H. Lawrence*, I, 377.

63. D. H. Lawrence, *Women in Love* (New York: Modern Library, n.d.), p. 394.

64. D. H. Lawrence, *Aaron's Rod* (New York: Thomas Seltzer, 1922), p. 95.

65. *Ibid.*, p. 31.

66. *Ibid.*, p. 134.

67. Ferenczi, *Further Contributions to the Theory and Technique of Psychoanalysis*, p. 279.

68. D. H. Lawrence, *Lady Chatterley's Lover* (New York: Grove Press, 1957), p. 261.

69. D. H. Lawrence, *The Plumed Serpent* (London: Martin Secker, 1926), pp. 451–52.

70. Nehls, *A Composite Biography of D. H. Lawrence*, II, 204.

71. The most recent collection of Lawrence's letters (Harry T. Moore [ed.], *The Collected Letters of D. H. Lawrence* [New York: Viking Press, 1962]) appeared after this book had gone to press. It contains a number of hitherto unpublished letters written in the weeks immediately following Lawrence's meeting and subsequent elopement with Frieda Lawrence, who was then married to Ernest Weekley. The letters deserve what brief mention I can give them since they provide an interesting cor-

roboration of affinities I had speculatively established between Lawrence's life and that pageant of passion, rivalry, violence, and atonement which his principals perform in almost all his fiction.

I have suggested that "The Old Adam," while it is not a major work, comes perhaps closest to describing the psychic undertones of Lawrence's rivalry with Ernest Weekley and his attraction toward Frieda. The letters confirm me in that suggestion and suggest further that the fictional representations of physical struggles to the death, as we find them in *Sons and Lovers,* "The Prussian Officer," *and* "The Old Adam" (all of which were in the process of composition during this time), find their practical basis in the relationship between Lawrence and his rival, Ernest Weekley.

Three familiar strains mingle in Lawrence's letters on this subject: a generous, but morbid solicitude for Ernest Weekley, which culminates in unequivocal contempt; a sense of his relationship and impending marriage to Frieda as a eucharistic experience; and, finally, a permissiveness toward Frieda, who had discovered another rival for Lawrence to hate and perhaps pity even while he was waiting to marry her—a permissiveness that savors wickedly, almost archly, the idea of sexual rivalry with other men and Frieda's identity as the "unconventional" *madonna puttana,* the "wet nurse," as he calls her, to still another fledgling lover.

In a letter to Edward Garnett (29 April 1912; I, 109), Lawrence writes about Ernest Weekley: "He is a middle class, gentlemanly man, in whom the brute can leap up. He is forty-six, and has been handsome, is usually ironic, pessimistic, and cynical, nice. I like him. He will hate me, but really he likes me at the bottom." A few weeks later Lawrence's ambivalences toward Weekley had resolved themselves in a dream. To Frieda he writes: "I dreamed Ernest was frantically furiously wild with me—I won't tell you the details—and then he calmed down, and I had to comfort him" (?9 May 1912; I, 116). Two years later the relationship with Weekley had run its course, perhaps to transfer itself to John Middleton Murry, to whom Lawrence now writes (3 April 1914; I, 270): "Her [Frieda's] old figurehead of a husband plays marionette Moses, then John Halifax, Gentleman, then Othello, then a Maupassant hero tracking down his victims. . . . He is a fool."

To Frieda immediately after her flight to Germany, Lawrence writes about their marriage in tones of breathless and innocent expectation (?15 May 1912; I, 121): "I know in my heart 'here's my marriage.' It feels rather terrible—because it is a great thing in my life—it is *my life*—I am a bit awe-inspired— I want to get used to it." Yet the next day, alluding apparently to Frieda's being attracted to another man, Lawrence is all Parisian magnanimity (To Frieda, 16 May 1912; I, 122): "If you want H——, or anybody, have him." And the next day his sympathies are all with H——: "Poor H——, poor devil! *Vous le croquez bien entre les dents.* . . . I think you're rather horrid to H——. You make him more babified—baby-fed. Or shall you leave him more manly?" (To Frieda, ?17 May 1912; I, 123).

BIBLIOGRAPHY

WORKS BY D. H. LAWRENCE

Aaron's Rod. New York: Thomas Seltzer, 1922.
Assorted Articles. New York: Alfred A. Knopf, 1930.
England My England. New York: Thomas Seltzer, 1922.
Fantasia of the Unconscious. London: William Heinemann, 1937.
The First Lady Chatterley. New York: Dial Press, 1944.
Lady Chatterley's Lover. New York: Grove Press, 1957.
The Lost Girl. New York: Thomas Seltzer, 1921.
The Man Who Died. The New Classics Series. New York: Alfred A. Knopf, 1928.
A Modern Lover. London: Martin Secker, 1934.
The Phoenix. New York: Viking Press, 1936.
The Plumed Serpent. London: Martin Secker, 1926.
The Prussian Officer. New York: Huebsch, 1917.
Psychoanalysis and the Unconscious. New York: Thomas Seltzer, 1921.
The Rainbow. New York: Modern Library, n.d.
Sons and Lovers. New York: Harper and Brothers, 1951.
The White Peacock. Hamburg: Albatross, 1932.
The Woman Who Rode Away. New York: Alfred A. Knopf, 1930.
Women in Love. New York: Modern Library, n.d.

OTHER REFERENCES

Aldington, Richard. *Portrait of a Genius, But* . . . . London: William Heinemann, 1950.

Brett, Dorothy. *Lawrence and Brett*. London: Martin Secker, 1933.

Carswell, Catherine. *Savage Pilgrimage*. London: Chatto and Windus, 1932.

Davies, Rhys. "D. H. Lawrence in Bandol," *Horizon*, II (October, 1940), 191–208.

Durrell, Lawrence. *Balthazar*. New York: Dutton and Co., 1958.

E. T. *D. H. Lawrence: A Memoir*. New York: Knight, 1936.

Eliot, T. S. *After Strange Gods*. London: Faber and Faber, 1934.

———. *Selected Essays*. New York: Harcourt-Brace and Co., 1932.

Ellis, Havelock. *Studies in the Psychology of Sex*. Philadelphia: F. A. Davis, 1928.

Ferenczi, Sandor. *Further Contributions to the Theory and Technique of Psychoanalysis*, translated by J. Suttie. London: Hogarth Press, 1926.

———. *Sex in Psychoanalysis*, translated by Ernest Jones. New York: Dover Publications, 1956.

Freud, Sigmund. *The Standard Edition of the Complete Psychological Works of Sigmund Freud*, translated from the German under the general editorship of James Strachey in collaboration with Anna Freud. London: Hogarth Press, 1955–61.

Gregory, Horace. *Pilgrim of the Apocalypse*. New York: Viking Press, 1933.

Hoffman, Frederick J. *Freudianism and the Literary Mind*. Baton Rouge: Louisiana State University Press, 1945.

———, and Harry Thornton Moore (eds.) *The Achievement of D. H. Lawrence*. Norman: University of Oklahoma Press, 1953.

Huxley, Aldous (ed.). *The Letters of D. H. Lawrence*. 1st ed. London: William Heinemann, 1932.

Jones, Ernest. *Hamlet and Oedipus*. New York: W. W. Norton and Co., 1949.

———. *The Life and Works of Sigmund Freud*. New York: Basic Books, 1959.

Jung, C. G. *Psychology of the Unconscious*, translated by B. M. Hinkle. New York: Dodd, Mead and Co., 1952.

Keiser, Sylvan. "Body Ego during Orgasm," *Psychoanalytic Quarterly*, XXI (April, 1952), 153–56.

Kenmare, Dallas. *Fire-bird: A Study of D. H. Lawrence*. London: Barrie, 1951.

Kingsmill, Hugh. *D. H. Lawrence*. London, Methuen, 1938.

Lawrence, Ada. *Young Lorenzo*. Florence: Orioli, 1931.

Lawrence, Frieda. *Not I but the Wind*. New York: Viking Press, 1934.

Leavis, F. R. *D. H. Lawrence*. Cambridge, Eng.: Minority Press, 1930.

———. *For Continuity*. Cambridge, Eng.: Minority Press, 1933.

Luhan, Mabel Dodge. *Lorenzo in Taos*. London: Martin Secker, 1933.

Moore, Harry Thornton. *The Intelligent Heart: The Story of D. H. Lawrence*. New York: Farrar, Straus and Young, 1954.

———. *The Life and Works of D. H. Lawrence*. New York: Twayne Publishers, 1951.

——— (ed.). *The Collected Letters of D. H. Lawrence*. New York: Viking Press, 1962.

Murry, John Middleton. *Son of Woman*. London: Jonathan Cape, 1931.

Nehls, Edward (ed.). *A Composite Biography of D. H. Lawrence*. Madison: University of Wisconsin Press, 1958. Vols. I–III.

Schorer, Mark. "Technique as Discovery," *Hudson Review*, I (Spring, 1948), 67–87.

Spender, Stephen. *The Destructive Element*. London: Jonathan Cape, 1935.

Tindall, William York. *D. H. Lawrence and Susan His Cow*. New York: Columbia University Press, 1939.

Tiverton, Father William. *D. H. Lawrence and Human Existence*. New York: Philosophical Library, 1951.

Troy, William. "The D. H. Lawrence Myth," *Partisan Review*, IV (January, 1938), 2, 3–13.

Yeats, William Butler (trans.). "Oedipus the King," in *Greek Plays in Modern Translation*, edited by Dudley Fitts. New York: Dial Press, 1947.

INDEX

The text of this book was set in 10-pt. Linotype Electra and the display in 18-pt. Monotype Deepdene by Westcott & Thomson, Inc., Philadelphia. Offset printing by Malloy Lithographing, Inc., Ann Arbor, Michigan. Binding by P. F. Pettibone & Company, Chicago. The book was designed by Dianne Weiss.